Chasing the Win

The Hidden Psychology
of Gambling Addiction

By
Alexander C. Blackwell

Chasing the Win

The Hidden Psychology
of Gambling Addiction

Table of Contents

Introduction

The human fascination with risk and chance has persisted through the ages, manifesting in endeavors that compel individuals to tempt fate or ride on the whims of probability. From ancient dice games to contemporary online slots, gambling presents a unique allure that can capture the minds and hearts of many. Whether seeking a quick thrill, a momentary escape, or even profound transformation, people of all walks are drawn to these games of chance.

Why does gambling hold such a potent sway over us? To answer this, one must delve into the psychological currents and emotional underpinnings that make an irresistible pull. At its core, gambling is not merely an act of wagering money but rather an intricate dance between anticipation and reward. It taps into primal parts of our brain, igniting pathways that thirst for novelty and excitement, creating a rollercoaster of emotion and impulse.

A major player in this intricate dance is our brain's reward system, specifically the dopamine pathways. This neurotransmitter is synonymous with pleasure and satisfaction, coursing through the mind like a triumphant fanfare when we engage in activities perceived as rewarding. Gambling exploits this reward system, effectively rewiring sensations of gratification and excitement into a potent psychological blend that can, for some, lead to addiction.

Such addiction is not a mere consequence of moral failing or lack of self-control, but rather a confluence of neurological, psychological, and social factors. It's a behavior pattern that gradually steals autonomy, overshadowing decisions until what was once an entertaining hobby becomes an all-consuming habit. The path from casual curiosity to dependence is often subtle but destructive, leaving a trail of emotional distress and disarray.

Understanding the psychological landscape of gambling addiction requires a multidimensional approach, considering mental, emotional, and even cultural influences that contribute to its development. As society changes, so too does the nature of gambling, particularly with the advent of technology that has revolutionized the landscape with online casinos and mobile betting. This transformation introduces new challenges and questions about accessibility and regulation, often leaving vulnerable individuals exposed to greater risk.

Traditional values and cultural norms also play significant roles in shaping gambling behaviors. What is perceived as a social pastime in one culture may be viewed as a moral pitfall in another. Thus, one must consider these perspectives to fully grasp the nuances of gambling addiction and develop strategies that resonate across diverse populations.

Likewise, the societal implications extend beyond the individual, touching on familial dynamics, economic repercussions, and even public health concerns. As gambling addiction escalates, it reverberates through one's social circle, drawing in loved ones who struggle to navigate the uncertainty and pain that often accompany addiction. Yet, amidst the turmoil, there exists a potential for recovery, for change, and for a future where the chains of addiction are broken.

The path to recovery is fraught with challenges, requiring a profound metamorphosis supported by therapeutic approaches and a strong support network. Empowering those affected with the knowledge and tools to withstand the compulsion is a crucial step toward long-term healing and resilience. Recovery is a testament to human strength and the capacity for change, underscoring the importance of hope and determination.

Addiction prevention demands community involvement and comprehensive education to build resilience against these psychological traps. It also calls for robust policy and regulation to ensure responsible gaming environments that prioritize player welfare over profit. By fostering awareness and understanding, communities and individuals can strike a balance—enabling the enjoyment of games without succumbing to their perilous allure.

The journey to comprehend gambling addiction is one of empathy, insight, and discovery, unraveling the depth of human psychology while challenging the societal structures that sustain it. Through research and continued dialogue, one aims to illuminate this shadowed path, encouraging a shift in perceptions and fostering environments conducive to healing and support. This book embarks on such a journey, with the hope of shedding light on a pervasive issue and charting new avenues for prevention, treatment, and recovery. Together, let us navigate the intricate maze of the mind where chance and choice converge.

Chapter 1:
The Allure of Risk

As the sun dips below the horizon, the symphony of slot machines softly fills the air, each chime striking a chord deep within the soul of a gambler. This is where the dance with risk begins, where individuals are captivated not only by glittering prospects but also by the primal thrill that courses through their veins. The gamble is more than a mere game; it's an intricate web weaving together the promise of reward with the intoxicating pull of uncertainty. It's here, in this delicate balance, that the allure of risk seduces the mind, tugging at the brain's reward system like an insistent tide. For many, it's an escape into a world where the roll of the dice or spin of the wheel recharts the predictable map of daily life, offering a tantalizing glimpse of control and mastery over fate. This powerful cocktail of chance and choice hints at untapped potential and the primal desire for something greater, something beyond the mundane, and therein lies the potent allure that can gently tug someone into murky waters.

Understanding the Thrill

What pushes a person to the edge, teetering between exhilaration and peril? This dance along the precipice is the heart of what makes risk alluring. Humans seem hardwired to seek experiences that quicken the pulse and stir emotions, a penchant for risk rooted deep within our psyche. At its core lies a complex interplay of biology, psychology, and situational context, all converging to shape this enigmatic attraction.

From ancient times, taking risks has been crucial for survival, allowing early humans to explore, hunt, and seek new opportunities. This ancestral necessity may have hardwired an inclination for risk-taking into our DNA, transforming it into a pursuit not just for survival, but for an adrenaline-fueled exhilaration. This mixture of excitement and anticipation creates an emotional high that can be incredibly addictive.

For those who gamble, this thrill is not just about the potential monetary gain; it's about the rush, the stylish dance with uncertainty. The uncertain outcomes of games of chance provoke an array of emotions: hope, fear, excitement, and anxiety, all tightly interwoven. These emotions fuel not only the interest in gambling but also the desire to experience the unpredictable nature of life in a controlled environment. Variety and unpredictability make gambling an attractive pastime for many individuals who crave excitement.

But why do some people chase this thrill more than others? The answer might lie in individual differences in personality and perception. Some people are naturally more risk-inclined, characterized by traits such as high sensation-seeking and openness to experience. These individuals tend to see risk differently—not as something to be feared, but as an opportunity for reward. For them, the thrill is not only about winning but also about the experience itself. This mindscape elevates the enjoyment of uncertainty and embraces the unknown.

Add to this the social and contextual aspects, and the allure deepens. Casinos, with their bright lights and lively atmosphere, amplify the thrill, providing both a physical and social space that intensifies the experience. The communal aspect of gambling—being surrounded by others caught up in the same pursuit—can foster a heightened sense of excitement. Social interactions can also serve to reinforce risk-taking behavior, as gamblers share their wins and losses, building a collective sense of anticipation and tension.

Another key element linked to the thrill is the disruption of everyday monotony. Gambling offers an escape, a break from routine that injects an element of unpredictability into the mundane. It's a contrast to the stability and order that govern most of life's activities. For some, the temporary detachment from reality becomes a cherished part of the experience, offering a reprieve from responsibilities and an indulgence in the unknown.

The environment in which gambling takes place adds layers to its appeal. The design of casinos and online gaming platforms is tailored to enhance the gamer's sense of thrill. From flashing lights and engaging sounds to strategically placed mirrors and curvature, casinos are built to entice. In online spaces, the thrill is crafted through interactive and immersive interfaces that hold players' attention and draw them deeper into the experience. These environments are crafted to maximize emotional engagement, with every element designed with the patron's pleasure at heart.

Risk-taking in gambling is also closely tied to perception of control. Feeling a sense of control in games of chance augments the thrill by making outcomes feel personal and attainable. Even though outcomes are largely dictated by randomness, the illusion of control can make the pursuit more enticing, as individuals believe they're influenced by their own skill or strategy. Thus, the perception of control and skill can be a mediating factor that intensifies the perceived thrill of gambling.

Moreover, cultural attitudes toward risk play a significant role in shaping its allure. Societies where risk-taking is celebrated and revered may encourage individuals to embrace the thrill of gambling more readily. In contrast, cultures that view risk more conservatively may produce individuals who find the thrill less appealing or even perceive it as reckless behavior. The cultural lens through which gambling is viewed can either amplify or diminish its appeal, coloring individual perceptions and experiences.

Psychologically, the thrill derived from gambling can act as a powerful reinforcement mechanism. Each exhilarating experience, each near-miss, and each small victory creates a feedback loop, reinforcing the behavior and heightening the desire to repeat the experience. Over time, the thrill becomes less a momentary sensation and more an ingrained part of a person's motivations, driving them further into the cycle of gambling behavior.

Understanding the intricate layers of thrill that fuel gambling addiction requires dissecting the motivations and emotions that accompany the process. Is it the escapism, the community, the perception of skill, or simply the physiological rush that draws people in? Each gambler's answer may differ, but the common thread remains: a potent combination of factors that make gambling a deeply enticing pursuit for many.

Yet, in seeking out these moments of thrill, the line between enjoyment and compulsion can become easily blurred. For some, the pursuit of thrill may devolve into a relentless chase, where the excitement becomes not just a pastime but a necessity. Recognizing these nuances is critical to understanding not only the allure of risk but its potential pitfalls as well.

Addressing this thrilling allure through a nuanced lens of both fascination and caution allows for a broader comprehension of the ways in which gambling captures our attention and alters behavior. This understanding is crucial for professionals seeking to demystify gambling addiction and provide effective prevention and recovery strategies. By peeling back the layers of the thrilling experience, we uncover the psychological underpinnings that fuel the cycle of gambling addiction and, in doing so, open pathways to deeper insight and intervention.

Risk and Reward in the Brain

The human brain is a complex and extraordinary organ, constantly weighing risks and rewards in a seamless dance that governs not just survival but the pursuit of pleasure. When it comes to gambling, understanding how our brains are attracted to risk is a powerful insight into why gambling can be so addictive. It's a compelling narrative where biology and behavior intersect, shaping our decisions in ways we're only beginning to comprehend.

At the core of this relationship between risk and reward lies the brain's reward system, a network of structures that includes the ventral tegmental area, nucleus accumbens, and prefrontal cortex. These parts are central in processing and reinforcing rewarding stimuli. When a potential reward is anticipated, dopamine—a neurotransmitter associated with pleasure and reward—flows through these circuits, creating feelings of excitement and anticipation. This neural activity is akin to the spark that lights the fire of gambling thrill.

Consider the moment before a roulette wheel stops or the tension in waiting for the final slot machine reel. That thrill at the intersection of suspense and potential gain is where dopamine plays its enchanting role. It primes us to take action, driving the desire to wager and to experience the associated highs. Herein lies part of the allure of risk— the brain's reward system subtly but powerfully conditions behaviors that enhance these feelings of satisfaction and pleasure.

Yet, caution must be exercised as this very system can lead individuals down the path of addiction. The brain, in its quest to maximize reward, can become fixated on the highs of gambling, prompting repeated behaviors despite negative consequences. In some people, this manifests as a compulsion to gamble, where the risk is overshadowed by the intoxicating prospect of reward. Despite frequent losses, the brain may still anticipate a reward, perpetuating a cycle that is hard to break.

Interestingly, risk-taking itself is not inherently negative. Evolutionarily, the propensity to take risks has likely contributed to human innovation and survival. Those who took calculated risks opened new doors for themselves and for society. However, in modern contexts, especially where gambling is concerned, this trait can become maladaptive. The shift occurs when the balance tilts from rewarding exploration to compulsive behavior.

Understanding this balance is key in developing effective strategies for managing gambling behaviors. It involves recognizing how individual differences and environmental factors may influence each person's balance of risk and reward. For instance, genetic predispositions or early life experiences may alter dopamine receptors' sensitivity, further complicating the picture.

Cognitive psychology adds another layer by explaining how our interpretations of risk and reward drive decision-making. Concepts like loss aversion—the idea that losses loom larger than gains—demonstrate how our mental frameworks might skew rational decision-making in gambling scenarios. Often, gamblers experience 'near-miss' events, which activate similar brain pathways as actual wins, further intoxicating the reward-seeking process.

This knowledge underscores the importance of targeted interventions in gambling addiction. By identifying how the brain processes risk and reward, therapy can better address maladaptive patterns. Cognitive-behavioral strategies, for instance, aim to recalibrate the brain's judgments and responses to risk, helping individuals build resilience against the temptations of gambling.

The pursuit of risk for potential reward is an inherent part of human nature. It's the reason why gambling holds such a strong allure, presenting both a challenge and an opportunity for those struggling with its grip. Navigating this terrain requires understanding that risk and reward are more than just economic terms; they're deeply embedded in our neurological and psychological fabric.

Ultimately, shedding light on the brain's role in processing risk and reward doesn't just help those with gambling problems; it enriches our understanding of human behavior at large. These insights pave the way for creating healthier relationships with risk, not just in gambling but in life's myriad decisions. The blend of excitement, anticipation, and decision-making that drives us toward risky endeavors is an intrinsic part of the human experience—a facet of our nature that, when understood, can be harnessed constructively.

Chapter 2:
The Science of Chance

In the intricate realm of gambling, the science of chance plays a pivotal role, shaping perceptions and drive. Though it seems straightforward, understanding probability often entangles gamblers in a web of misconceptions and false hopes. Many gamblers fall prey to cognitive distortions and misguided beliefs, convincing themselves they can predict or control random outcomes. This illusion of control, fueled by past near-wins and superstitious rituals, lures individuals into a cycle of misguided decision-making. The human brain, in its quest for patterns, tends to misunderstand the laws of probability, leading to overestimation of winning chances. Such misunderstandings can catalyze the dangerous allure of gambling, setting the stage for addictive behaviors as gamblers chase elusive victories. Recognizing these fundamental misinterpretations is crucial in unraveling the psychological depth of gambling addiction and forging paths toward realistic perception and recovery.

Probability Misunderstandings

Human beings have an uncanny ability to find patterns, even where none exist. This is both a blessing and a curse when it comes to gambling. Misunderstandings about probability can be a key driver of addiction, making it crucial to understand the misconceptions surrounding it. The average mind is not wired to intuitively grasp the laws of probability, leading many to enter casinos or betting parlors under false assumptions. Nowhere is this more evident than in the "gambler's fallacy," the belief that past events can influence future outcomes in games of chance.

This fallacy often manifests in the conviction that a slot machine "is due" for a win after a string of losses. However, each spin of the reels operates independently, unaffected by previous outcomes. Despite this, the human brain struggles to let go of the notion that the universe has a sense of balance that will inevitably bring a win. Understanding how randomized events truly work is a significant step in breaking the grip of this fallacy.

But the gambler's fallacy is just the tip of the iceberg. Another common misunderstanding involves the concept of "lucky streaks." People often believe they're on a winning streak, and that this streak will continue indefinitely. These perceptions are fueled by a cognitive bias known as the "hot-hand fallacy," which leads individuals to expect ongoing success based on prior wins. While luck can seem palpable in the heat of the moment, recognizing that each event in gambling is standalone can help dispel these dangerous illusions.

Complex psychological mechanisms often enhance these probability misunderstandings. Cognitive biases such as confirmation bias further complicate the picture. Gamblers may remember and highlight wins while downplaying losses. Selective memory allows individuals to construct a narrative that justifies continued gambling, ensuring that their beliefs in these streaks seem reasonable, even rational.

In addition to cognitive biases, emotional states heavily sway one's understanding of probability. Heightened emotions can cloud judgment, making individuals more susceptible to distorted views of chance. For example, a gambler in distress might grasp at any seemingly positive outcome, interpreting it as a sign to persist. By addressing the emotional components tied to these misunderstandings, there's potential to diminish their power over decision-making.

Consider the concept of probability in a coin toss—a simple 50/50 chance. Even after multiple flips resulting in heads, the likelihood of the next flip being tails remains 50%. Yet, despite the apparent simplicity, when faced with a sequence of several heads in a row, many begin to expect tails. This stems from another error: the "law of small numbers," where people mistakenly believe small sample sizes will resemble larger statistical trends.

Educational strategies aimed at demystifying probability can play a vital role in addiction prevention. Teaching individuals the principles of randomness and the independence of events could alter ingrained misconceptions. Visual aids and interactive simulations can help demonstrate these principles in a tangible way. By fostering a culture of awareness around these errors, we can reduce the risky behaviors associated with them.

Moreover, understanding probability misconceptions is not just crucial for individual gamblers; it has broader implications for society. Casinos, lotteries, and betting companies often profit from these misunderstandings, designing games that exploit cognitive biases. Public policies could integrate better educational initiatives to warn against these dangers, creating a safer environment for potential gamblers.

Addressing these misunderstandings extends into therapeutic practices as well. Therapists can introduce cognitive-behavioral techniques aimed at correcting faulty reasoning about probability. Insight into these errors can be empowering for the individual, allowing them to slowly reclaim control over their thought processes and future decisions.

Recognizing these misunderstandings in oneself may take time and honest reflection. It involves accepting vulnerability to errors and biases. Yet, this acceptance can be freeing, opening pathways to more informed and conscious decision-making. By embracing a more accurate view of how chance operates, individuals can build more resistance to the seductive pull of gambling.

In the end, rooting out probability misunderstandings is an ongoing journey. Though the misconception is deeply etched into human cognition, awareness and education provide hope. Through a combination of systemic changes, individual efforts, and technological interventions, it is possible to lessen the grip of these errors, paving the way for healthier interactions with risk and chance.

The Illusion of Control

Within the science of chance, a peculiar phenomenon known as "the illusion of control" emerges. It's a psychological condition where individuals believe they have influence over outcomes that are, in reality, largely dictated by chance. This illusion is not merely a form of self-deception but rather a deeply ingrained cognitive bias that can drive the behaviors of those engaged in gambling. The illusion often manifests when a gambler believes that throwing the dice in a certain way or choosing specific lottery numbers can somehow affect the outcome. This perception, while unfounded, can be powerful enough to draw individuals back to the gambling table time and again.

The concept stems from what psychologists have identified as "control heuristics" — mental shortcuts that humans use to make sense of uncertainty. These heuristics lead us to overestimate our ability to influence events, particularly in situations that involve personal choice or require some form of skill. In gambling, the illusion of control is especially deceptive because it mimics the skills and decision-making we rely on in our daily lives. When gamblers experience a win, no matter how infrequent, they often attribute it to their own actions rather than pure luck. This false sense of competence can perpetuate gambling behavior, fostering addiction.

Research underscores that this illusion is not limited to gambling alone; it can occur in various aspects of life where luck is misconstrued as skill. However, in a casino setting, the environment itself is engineered to enhance this illusion. Games often involve elements that mimic skill-based activities, such as card games or sports betting, which require decisions and strategies. Here, players mistakenly believe their expertise is steering their success, despite the random nature of outcomes. This deception is cunning, as it gives gamblers a sense of mastery and engagement, deepening the psychological grip of gambling addiction.

Interestingly, human beings have a natural tendency to seek control over their environment. Historically, this trait has helped us survive by anticipating and managing challenges. Yet, in modern contexts like betting, it facilitates an emotional misinterpretation. Being in control can be exhilarating, providing a high similar to that induced by substances, reinforcing the cycle of gambling. The promise of control, however illusory, becomes intertwined with the gambler's sense of self-worth and personal efficacy.

The illusion is further compounded by what behavioral scientists call "near miss" experiences. These are situations where an outcome is close to a winning one, pushing the gambler to feel they are on the verge of success due to their "skill." These near misses create a false sense of proximity to a win, triggering dopamine responses in the brain akin to actual wins. This reaction can heighten the belief in personal control over chance outcomes, pulling the gambler further down the path of addiction.

Despite its deceptive nature, the illusion of control offers valuable insight into strategies for recovery and prevention. By understanding this cognitive bias, therapists and counselors can develop targeted interventions that challenge these faulty beliefs. Strategies such as cognitive-behavioral therapy focus on altering these perceptions, helping individuals distinguish between skill-based activities and those governed by chance. Educating gamblers about the true nature of randomness can demystify these illusory control beliefs, gradually undermining the psychological allure of gambling.

Moreover, fostering awareness about the illusion of control can serve as a protective factor against the onset of gambling problems. Educational programs that highlight the randomness inherent in gambling games could disarm the power of this cognitive bias. By unpacking the myth of control, potential gamblers might approach these activities with a more realistic understanding, reducing the risk of developing addictive behaviors.

Similarly, debunking the notion of control is crucial for developing prevention strategies, especially in young people who are particularly susceptible to illusions molded by peer pressure and media influences. Creating a narrative that starkly contrasts the fantasy of control with the reality of chance can empower individuals with the knowledge to resist these psychological traps.

In a broader sense, the illusion of control highlights the intricate connection between psychology and behavior within the realm of gambling. It emphasizes the necessity of acknowledging these biases, not only for those experiencing addiction but also for professionals working to combat this issue. As we dig deeper into the science of chance, we uncover how perceptions shape reality and how awareness can pave the way for healing and empowerment.

Chapter 3:
The Brain's Reward System

In this chapter, we dive into the intricacies of the brain's reward system to unravel why gambling can become a consuming compulsion for some. The brain is wired to seek out rewards, and when a person gambles, it engages this system by releasing dopamine, a neurotransmitter that fosters feelings of pleasure and satisfaction. This powerful neurochemical reaction is what instigates the thrilling "high" that can keep individuals returning for more, despite the odds stacked against them. As slot machines ring and cards flip, the anticipation of a possible win triggers these dopamine surges, creating a loop of expectation and reward. It's this biological dance that can lead pathways straight to addiction. Yet, understanding how the brain's reward circuitry functions allows us to shed light on why certain patterns emerge and provides vital insight into curbing the potential spiral into addiction. By demystifying these mechanisms, we arm ourselves to tackle the root cause of gambling addiction and offer glimmers of hope for breaking free from its grip.

How Dopamine Drives Behavior

In the intricate landscape of the human brain, dopamine plays a pivotal role as a chemical messenger. It's not just a molecule; dopamine is the essence of drive and motivation, acting as the fuel for our desires and actions. Its importance cannot be overstated in the context of understanding gambling addiction. By exploring how dopamine influences behavior, we unravel one of the most significant factors that compels someone toward the allure of gambling, often with disastrous consequences.

Dopamine is often associated with the experience of pleasure, but this is a simplistic view. Instead, it's more accurate to think of dopamine as a mediator of expectation and reward, a crucial player in the brain's reward system. When you engage in activities deemed pleasurable or rewarding, like eating your favorite food or achieving a goal, your brain releases dopamine. This release doesn't just make you feel good; it creates a neural "memory" of this pleasurable event, setting the stage for future behaviors. Now, you might wonder, what exactly makes dopamine such a powerful driver of behavior, especially in gambling?

The story begins in the brain's reward pathway, particularly the ventral tegmental area (VTA) and the nucleus accumbens. These areas light up when you're about to experience something rewarding. As dopamine floods these regions, it enhances your focus, motivation, and memory associated with the event. For gamblers, this neural activation occurs as they anticipate a win. The act of placing a bet becomes intertwined with these dopamine releases, creating a powerful cycle of anticipation and reward.

Interestingly, it's not just winning that releases dopamine; the mere expectation or uncertainty of a reward can also trigger its release. This is where gambling becomes dangerously captivating. Unlike predictable rewards found in many daily activities, gambling offers intermittent, unpredictable rewards, which are particularly effective at increasing dopamine levels. This uncertainty makes the reward feel even more rewarding. Essentially, the "high" of gambling lies not just in winning but in the thrill of anticipating a potential win, even if it's unlikely.

The mechanism has an evolutionary basis. Our ancestors needed this dopamine-driven anticipation to motivate behaviors necessary for survival, like chasing prey or gathering food despite not always being successful. In modern society, however, this same mechanism can ensnare individuals within the confines of compulsive gambling. While a win is uncertain, the brain's biochemistry doesn't differentiate—it's perpetually driven by the hope of potentially lucrative outcomes, fueled by dopamine.

A key insight into how dopamine affects behavior is in its influence on decision-making. When you're under the sway of a dopamine release, you might prioritize immediate rewards over long-term consequences. This can lead a person to disregard rational thought processes and apparent risks, compelling them to take increasingly bolder chances. For a gambler, it becomes a game of 'one more chance,' propelled by the biochemical lure of dopamine, pushing them to pretend that just one more wager could finally be the one that pays off.

Moreover, chronic exposure to gambling and the associated dopamine surges can alter the brain's chemistry, leading to changes in the way it responds to natural rewards and stressors. Over time, someone addicted to gambling may find less joy in activities that used to bring satisfaction. This results from the brain's tolerance to the high levels of dopamine experienced during gambling, requiring more and more stimulation to achieve the same level of reward. This is why gambling addiction can seem to consume an individual's entire life—they need to gamble not only for potential winnings but to experience the dopamine-driven satisfaction.

Withdrawal is another challenge. When a person attempts to cut back or stop gambling, the absence of dopamine-induced highs can cause significant discomfort. This deficit can manifest as anxiety, depression, and irritability—creating a painful rebound that often leads back to gambling as a means to restore dopamine equilibrium. This vicious cycle reinforces the compulsive nature of gambling addiction and underscores why it's so challenging to overcome without proper intervention and support.

Understanding the role of dopamine in driving behavior offers invaluable insights into the mechanisms of gambling addiction. It highlights how the brain's design, beneficial in contexts of survival and decision-making, can be maladaptive in today's world of accessible and enticing gambling opportunities. Awareness of dopamine's influence and learning to cope with its effects is a crucial step for those seeking recovery from gambling addiction, making strategies like cognitive-behavioral therapy highly effective. This therapy helps individuals reframe their thinking, promoting healthy decision-making and building resilience against the allure of dopamine-driven gambling behavior.

The journey to overcoming gambling addiction isn't just about the absence of behavior; it's about reconditioning the brain's reward system. By developing healthier habits, individuals learn to derive pleasure and motivation from non-gambling activities, gradually reforming the brain's response to natural rewards. This reshaping is essential not only for breaking free from addiction but for regaining control over one's life, ensuring that dopamine serves its original purpose—helping you thrive rather than imprisoning you in the cyclical despair of addiction.

Pathways to Addiction

Understanding how gambling can become an addiction requires us to delve into the intricate mechanisms of the brain's reward system. At its core, addiction is often a dysregulation of this system, where the brain's natural pathways are hijacked by external stimuli, such as gambling. This hijacking is neither instantaneous nor uniform across individuals;

it manifests differently based on a complex interplay of biological, psychological, and social factors.

In the realm of neuroscience, dopamine is the key player that links the reward system to addictive behaviors. Dopamine is not just a "pleasure molecule," as commonly misunderstood, but rather a neurotransmitter involved in predicting rewards. When you gamble, dopamine levels surge not merely in response to winning but also in anticipation of a win. This anticipation is crucial; it creates a loop that fuels the desire to gamble, propelling the individual down a pathway toward addiction.

The process is deceptively gradual. Initially, gambling provides mild euphoria without significant consequences. For many, it's an occasional activity. But for others, the consistent engagement with gambling taps into a pathway of escalating cravings. As the brain adapts to frequent dopamine surges, desensitization occurs. The same gamble no longer provides the initial thrill, prompting individuals to pursue riskier bets or more frequent gambling episodes to achieve the desired effect. This escalation is a hallmark of the addictive pathway, analogous to how substance abuse can evolve.

Moreover, the brain's reward system doesn't function in isolation. It's part of a broader network that encompasses emotion and cognition. As one develops a gambling habit, the reward pathways often intertwine with emotional regulation systems. Stress, anxiety, and depression can intensify the appeal of gambling. Here, gambling becomes a maladaptive strategy for emotional escape rather than just a seeking of reward. This dual pathway—seeking reward and avoiding negative emotions—creates a robust cycle that fortifies the addiction.

Narratives of those addicted to gambling frequently reveal this duality. It's not just about the high of winning but also about numbing life's pressures or escaping from mental distress. The brain's attempts to self-medicate through gambling are misguided but powerful. As these pathways strengthen, neural real estate in the brain becomes increasingly dedicated to gambling-related thoughts and urges. This reorganization, characterized by enhanced neural connectivity in addictive pathways, makes quitting especially challenging.

Environmental cues play a significant role in reinforcing these pathways. Just as Pavlov's dogs salivated at the sound of a bell, gamblers may experience surges of craving when exposed to specific triggers. Be it the jingle of a slot machine, the ambiance of a casino, or even digital ads for online gambling. These stimuli can reignite dormant pathways, leading to relapse even after prolonged abstinence. Such conditioned responses are rooted deeply in the neural circuitry of addiction.

Understanding pathways to addiction also means recognizing genetic predispositions. Research has shown that some individuals are more susceptible to addiction due to genetic configurations that affect neurotransmitter systems and impulse control. While genetic risk factors don't doom one to addiction, they can significantly shift one's vulnerability when exposed to gambling environments. Familial patterns of addiction, particularly within first-degree relatives, highlight genetics' role in the backdrop of gambling problems.

Social and cultural influences further add layers to these pathways. For example, individuals growing up in environments where gambling is normalized or even glamorized may develop permissive attitudes towards it. The intersection of cultural values with individual vulnerabilities can accelerate one's journey from casual gambling to addiction. Societal expectations can sometimes mask these developmental signs, delaying identification and intervention.

Ultimately, pathways to addiction underscore a metamorphosis of the brain's reward infrastructure. Recognizing these pathways doesn't just aid in diagnosing addiction but also illuminates potential avenues for intervention. Therapeutic strategies often aim to recalibrate these pathways, helping individuals establish healthier reward systems and emotional coping mechanisms. Cognitive behavioral therapy, for instance, endeavors to break the cycle of maladaptive thoughts and behaviors, fostering new pathways that encourage sustainable recovery.

Recovery is not a linear process but a journey of re-mapping the brain's reward landscape. Understanding one's unique pathways to addiction can provide invaluable insights into tailored treatment approaches. It's a reminder that while the brain's pathways can be diverted into addiction, they can also be steered towards healing and resilience. As science unveils more about these pathways, hope emerges for more effective prevention and redemption strategies, illuminating the way forward for individuals ensnared by gambling addiction.

Chapter 4:
The Psychological Hook

The psychological grip of gambling often takes root through a series of complex emotional and cognitive triggers, which gamblers might not even notice until they are deeply enmeshed. At its core, the allure lies in its ability to blend uncertainty with the excitement of possible reward, creating a potent mix that resonates with an intrinsic human desire for novelty and challenge. This emotional tug is further tightened by reinforcement schedules that reward unpredictably, fueling compulsive behavior as individuals chase that elusive high. Simultaneously, gambling crafts an alternate reality, providing a temporary escape from life's pressures and personal challenges. This seductive illusion can solidify into a comforting habit, as the brain learns to associate gambling with momentary relief and pleasure, making it all the more difficult to step away. Understanding these hooks is essential for those looking to untangle themselves or others from the shadows of addiction, offering a pathway to awareness, prevention, and healing.

Reinforcement Schedules

At the heart of gambling addiction lies the intricate dance of reinforcement schedules. These schedules, whether they're fixed or variable, dictate how and when rewards are offered. They are a potent force, shaping behavior with the precision of a master sculptor crafting a work of art. With each pull of the lever or click of a button, the gambler becomes entwined in a pattern of anticipation and reward. It's a cycle that seems deceptively simple yet is deeply ingrained in the mechanics of addiction.

Reinforcement schedules are not just about the promise of reward; they're about the unpredictability of it. Variable reinforcement, where the outcome is uncertain and the rewards come at unpredictable intervals, is particularly powerful. It's the same principle that makes slot machines irresistible. A win might occur after three spins, or it might take three hundred, but each possibility entices the gambler to keep trying, just one more time. The occasional win is enough to maintain hope and engagement, fueling further plays and deeper entrenchment in the cycle.

In behavioral psychology, these reinforcement schedules are used to understand how behaviors are learned and maintained. For gamblers, the variable ratio schedule is especially effective. It creates a high rate of response, as the gambler doesn't know which spin will be the winning one, but they believe that the next one might be. This belief in possibility is what keeps players at the machines for hours on end, driven by the thought that the jackpot is just around the corner.

Fixed reinforcement schedules, on the other hand, offer rewards after a set number of actions or a fixed interval of time. While these are less common in gambling, they still play a role in fostering addictive behavior. Consider loyalty programs, where players earn points or rewards after a certain amount of play. These incentives reinforce continued gambling, as the player is motivated to play "just a bit more" to reach the next reward level.

The allure of variable reinforcement schedules is compounded by personal biases and misconceptions. Gamblers often fall prey to the gambler's fallacy, the erroneous belief that past outcomes affect future ones. This fallacy can create a false sense of control, making the unpredictability of variable reinforcement even more intoxicating. A string of losses might lead a gambler to believe that a win is "due," heightening their determination to continue despite mounting losses.

Understanding the psychological pull of reinforcement schedules offers a glimpse into why some individuals become ensnared in gambling's web. It's not just about the possibility of winning money; it's about the unpredictable nature of those wins. The rush of a surprise payout releases dopamine in the brain, reinforcing the behavior and making it more likely to be repeated. This cycle of expectation and reward becomes a powerful motivator, overriding logic and often leading to destructive patterns.

Breaking the grip of these reinforcement schedules is a key challenge in overcoming gambling addiction. Cognitive Behavioral Therapy (CBT) often emphasizes recognizing and altering thought patterns associated with gambling. By understanding how reinforcement schedules work, individuals can start to see through the illusion of control and randomness. It's a crucial step in reclaiming autonomy over one's actions and breaking the cycle of addiction.

Therapeutic interventions can also focus on developing alternative behaviors that provide similar reinforcement without the negative consequences. Introducing hobbies or activities that offer a sense of achievement and reward can help shift the focus away from gambling. The challenge is in finding activities that fulfill the same need for excitement and reward, but the investment is worthwhile for achieving long-term recovery.

Additionally, public education about the nature of reinforcement and its role in addiction can be a preventive measure. Awareness programs could explain how these schedules operate in gambling environments, helping potential gamblers understand the risks before they start. By dispelling myths about "lucky streaks" and educating about the underlying psychological mechanisms, society can take significant steps toward reducing the incidence of gambling addiction.

The interplay of reinforcement schedules in gambling addiction isn't just a topic for academic exploration; it's a vital aspect of understanding the lived experiences of those affected. Whether it's the compulsive pursuit of the next big win or the gradual spiraling into addiction, recognizing these patterns is a formidable weapon in combating the hold gambling can have over individuals.

For practitioners working with individuals struggling with gambling addiction, maintaining an understanding of these reinforcement processes is essential. They provide insights into the mind of the gambler—how they think, what drives them, and most importantly, how they can be supported through recovery.

The ultimate goal in addressing gambling addiction is not just to stop the behavior but to understand and restructure the underlying psychological framework that supports it. By unraveling the role of reinforcement schedules, we take one more step toward empowering individuals to break free from the grip of addiction, offering them a clearer path to recovery and a life beyond gambling.

Escaping Reality

The human mind craves relief from the burdens of daily life, and the allure of escapism often provides a temporary sanctuary from reality's demands. This quest for escape is a vital element in understanding the psychological hooks that bind individuals to gambling. The appeal lies not just in the possibility of financial gain but in the seductive promise of liberation from one's immediate surroundings, whether those surroundings are stressful, mundane, or unbearably predictable.

Gambling offers a seductive gateway into an alternate reality where the troubles of everyday life fade into the background. Each spin of the roulette wheel or shuffle of the deck creates a world brimming with potential and opportunity, altering an individual's perception, even if just for a fleeting moment. Escaping into this vivid world can be heavily intoxicating for the gambler who finds solace amidst the chaos of chance and stakes.

Consider the psychological transformation occurring during gambling sessions. The intense concentration and heightened state of arousal narrow an individual's focus until it excludes everything but the game. This tunnel vision creates a psychological bubble where worries and stressors have no entry. Within this bubble, gamblers find temporary respite, feeling liberated from responsibilities and emotional burdens.

Such moments of escape are meticulously designed features of gambling environments, characterized by sensory stimulation and strategic layout. Bright lights, enticing sounds, and the ceaseless merry-go-round of action are carefully orchestrated to immerse individuals fully. This immersive quality ensures that the mind is constantly engaged, leaving no room for external concerns or introspection. Every detail is tailored to sustain the illusion and deepen the experience of otherworldly immersion.

Yet it's crucial to recognize that this escape is temporary, and the repercussions of remaining tethered to it can be quite severe. As gamblers are drawn into these brief refuges, they may begin to avoid dealing with real-world issues. This avoidance can create a cycle where the individual increasingly relies on gambling as a primary means of coping. The escape offered by gambling turns into a trap, as the person becomes ensnared by the very activity meant to provide relief.

For some, gambling offers a break from the isolation or emotional pain felt in everyday life. It's not uncommon for those grappling with underlying issues—such as depression or anxiety—to turn to gambling as a form of self-medication. The adrenaline and dopamine released during a gambling session can temporarily soothe these emotional wounds, but this relief masks deeper problems, potentially exacerbating them over time.

Moreover, the highs and lows intrinsic to gambling experiences create an emotional rollercoaster, effectively drawing individuals deeper into its thrall. Wins spark joy and satisfaction, presenting a stark contrast to the monotony or discontentment that might characterize the gambler's daily life. Meanwhile, losses, while painful, promise the redemption of future potential wins, keeping hope alive and perpetuating the cycle of escape.

The phenomenon of escapism through gambling isn't isolated to any one type of person; it transcends demographics. From young people seeking distraction from academic pressure to adults wrestling with mid-life crises, the urge to find an alternative reality is a universal aspect of the human condition. This broad appeal makes understanding this escape crucial in addressing gambling addiction across various population segments.

Breaking the cycle of escapist gambling requires more than just a vow to cease gambling. It involves addressing the core issues that drive the desire to escape. Therapeutic interventions, such as cognitive-behavioral therapy, can help individuals recognize underlying triggers and develop healthier coping mechanisms. Through therapy, people learn to confront the realities they are avoiding rather than seeking temporary refuge in gambling.

Supporting loved ones on this journey is equally vital. Trust and understanding are crucial in helping those with gambling addiction feel secure enough to face reality. Families and friends can play a significant role by fostering a supportive environment where individuals feel safe to express their fears and anxieties without judgment. Such support serves as a counterbalance to the isolating pull of escapism.

While gambling offers a potent escape from reality, confronting and understanding the reasons behind this desire is critical for anyone seeking recovery. By delving into the psychological foundations that make gambling such an attractive mode of escapism, we can better equip individuals with the tools and strategies necessary to break free from these constraints and lead healthier, more sustainable lives. The key lies in transforming the narrative from one of avoidance to one of empowerment and resilience.

Chapter 5:
Early Signs of Addiction

Spotting the early signs of gambling addiction can be challenging yet crucial for prevention and recovery. Often, the first indicators are subtle, manifesting as changes in a person's behavior and routines. They might start to discuss gambling more frequently, with enthusiasm that borders on obsession. Personal relationships might suffer as the individual isolates themselves to gamble. Financial red flags, like unexplained expenses or borrowing money, can appear early on. As the compulsion grows, it seeps into their daily life, disrupting work or neglecting responsibilities. In this critical phase, understanding these warning signals can make a significant difference, helping to interrupt the spiral before gambling becomes entrenched as a destructive force. By recognizing these shifts in behavior, loved ones and professionals can offer timely interventions that pave the way to recovery, emphasizing that awareness is a powerful ally in combatting addiction.

Recognizing Warning Signals

Understanding the onset of gambling addiction requires keen insight into the subtle warning signals that often precede more noticeable compulsive behaviors. People may think that these signs are obvious, but addiction often tiptoes into a person's life, masked by excitement and the allure of potential winnings. It's in these initial stages that recognizing shifts in patterns or attitudes can make a significant difference, potentially redirecting a path before damage becomes irreversible.

The early signs of gambling addiction can manifest in various forms, beyond simply spending more time or money on gambling activities. One of the earliest indicators is preoccupation. Individuals may find themselves constantly thinking about their next betting opportunity or reliving past gambling experiences. This mental occupation often intrudes upon other daily activities, resulting in decreased productivity at work or disinterest in social functions, as their focus continually drifts back to the thrill of gambling.

Financial inconsistencies can also signal a brewing problem. At the start, these might seem like harmless "investments" with the hopeful belief of a substantial payoff. However, when someone starts to consistently borrow money, dip into savings, or neglect essential financial obligations to support their gambling, it's a clear warning that their relationship with gambling is unhealthy. Over time, this can spiral into a cycle of debt that becomes increasingly difficult to escape.

Behavioral changes, though often subtle, are critical indicators of addiction. A person who was once cheerful and outgoing may become irritable or withdrawn. Mood swings can become common; the highs of winning and the severe lows of losing can create an emotional rollercoaster. These mood shifts often result in tension within personal relationships, as family members or friends struggle to understand the sudden changes.

Moreover, these individuals might start to lie about their gambling habits, even when not directly questioned. This deceit isn't just about where they've been or what they've been doing, but extends to hiding evidence of their losses or the extent of their gambling. The need to cover up these actions only deepens the secrecy and isolation, further entrenching the cycle of addiction.

Another significant warning signal is the development of tolerance. Much like substance addiction, gambling addicts often require more intense gambling experiences or larger bets to attain the same level of excitement they once found in smaller wagers. This growing tolerance is a slippery slope, pushing them toward riskier behaviors that could result in disastrous financial and personal consequences.

The social ramifications of gambling addiction are profound. Those on this trajectory may begin distancing themselves from long-time friends who don't gamble, preferring the company of fellow gamblers who understand their "dedication" to the game. This social shift often serves as a reinforcement of their habits, inadvertently creating an environment where gambling is normalized and even encouraged.

Family members and close friends play a crucial role in identifying these warning signals, as they are usually the first to notice shifts in behavior or priorities. Open communication and a supportive environment can be instrumental in encouraging individuals to seek help early on. It's paramount for loved ones to approach the topic with empathy and understanding, rather than confrontation, to prevent defensive reactions that could push the individual further into denial.

Gambling addiction isn't just about losing money; it's about losing control. Recognizing the warning signals is a powerful step in reclaiming one's life. For professionals, awareness and education on these early signs can enhance intervention strategies. By implementing early identification methods and providing accessible resources, it's possible to steer individuals back towards stability before deeper harm occurs.

Recognizing these warning signals is the first defense against a devastating journey. Constant vigilance, coupled with understanding and support, can alter the course of an individual's path, guiding them away from addiction's grasp and toward healthier, more fulfilling pursuits.

Shifts in Behavior

In the early stages of gambling addiction, one of the earliest indicators often lies in the subtle shifts in behavior. These changes can be so gradual that they may go unnoticed by the individual and their loved ones. However, recognizing these early signs is crucial in addressing the addiction before it spirals out of control.

The first noticeable change frequently occurs in social behaviors. Individuals who once valued spending time with friends and family might begin to isolate themselves. Gambling starts to take precedence over social commitments and hobbies. They may cancel plans or consistently show up late, distracted by the need to gamble "just one more time."

An obsession with gambling further manifests in conversations. Friends and family might notice that discussions increasingly revolve around gambling—tales of near-wins, strategies, and the excitement of the game. This focus can become a repetitive theme in the gambler's dialogue, often at the expense of other interests.

As gambling becomes more central in a person's life, their everyday routines start to shift. They might begin to neglect responsibilities at work or at home. Performance may drop, deadlines might be missed, and there could be a noticeable lack of focus. Employers may be the first to notice this change, observing increased absenteeism or a lack of motivation in tasks previously handled with ease.

Financial behaviors also undergo significant alterations. Individuals may start to display an increasing concern for money, often accompanied by secrecy. They might become evasive about finances, hiding transactions or lying about where money is going. Drastic steps might be taken, such as selling personal belongings or borrowing large sums without a clear plan for repayment. This secretive nature can further isolate the individual from their support network.

Alongside social withdrawal, a shift in mood is often apparent. The emotional rollercoaster associated with gambling addiction can lead to irritability, anxiety, or even moments of euphoria when wins occur. However, these highs are typically short-lived and followed by deeper lows. These mood swings can strain relationships, leading to conflicts and further withdrawal.

Changes in behavior can also be seen in a person's routines and habits. Those in the grip of gambling addiction may become fixated on rituals associated with gambling, from frequent visits to gambling venues to developing superstitious behaviors that they believe will impact their luck. Over time, these rituals can intensify, further consuming the person's thoughts and actions.

The impact on physical health cannot be overlooked. Gamblers might neglect their health, skipping meals or losing sleep to chase the next bet. The stress of gambling and the financial pressures associated with it can also lead to more serious health issues, such as high blood pressure or gastrointestinal problems.

Among younger individuals, changes in behavior can be particularly pronounced. Youth may start to disregard academic responsibilities or abandon educational goals altogether. The lure of quick money and the excitement of gambling can overshadow the importance of long-term achievements.

For older individuals, the signs may appear in different patterns, such as increased visits to gambling establishments masked as social outings or engaging with online gambling platforms under the guise of pass-time activities. This can lead to financial decisions that jeopardize their savings, impacting not only their future but also that of their families.

In essence, these behavioral shifts serve as a cry for help, though the individual may not recognize it as such. It's vital that those close to the person respond with understanding, rather than judgment, to encourage acknowledgment and seek intervention. Early recognition and support can steer them towards recovery before the psychological hooks of gambling dig in too deep.

Understanding these shifts is more than merely observing changes; it's about seeing beneath the surface to the psychological transformations that accompany gambling addiction. The path to addiction is paved with patterns of behavior that gradually derail one's life, signifying how deeply the allure of risk and reward has rooted itself within them.

Chapter 6:
The Emotional Void

At the heart of many gambling addictions lies an emotional void, a chasm created by unmet emotional needs or unresolved psychological conflicts. For some, gambling becomes a refuge, a temporary escape from life's realities and emotional turmoil. It's not just the thrill of the game or the potential for financial gain that captivates them; it's the fleeting sense of validation and the illusion of control. This emotional escape, however, often masks deeper issues, where the initial relief quickly spirals into dependency. Understanding these emotional triggers is crucial in recognizing why individuals return to the casino floor, online platforms, or betting shops despite the risks. Identifying and addressing these emotional gaps can be pivotal, offering pathways to recovery and prevention by teaching healthier ways to cope with life's inherent challenges.

Gambling as Emotional Escape

In the silent corridors of the human mind, where solitude meets introspection, emotions weave a complex tapestry that can be both baffling and enlightening. It's in these shadows that the idea of gambling as an emotional escape finds its roots. People often seek refuge in activities that allow them to detach from their emotional turmoil. For many, gambling becomes more than a game of chance; it transforms into a sanctuary where fleeting relief from life's burdens can be found.

The decision to gamble isn't always about chasing thrills or winning money. For some, it's an effort to fill an emotional void, a gap where joy should reside but doesn't. The lights, sounds, and action of a casino, or even the virtual spin of an online slot, offer distractions that push aside loneliness, anxiety, and depression. Inside this frenetic world, the mind finds a temporary shield from reality, a momentary lapse in the incessant replay of negative emotions and stresses.

This escape mechanism isn't unique to gambling; it mirrors other behaviors like compulsive shopping or excessive video gaming. However, what sets gambling apart is its dual promise of distraction and potential reward. The brain's pleasure centers light up with the possibility of winning, even if reality offers no assurance. It's this glimmer of hope that turns a simple bet into a beacon of possibility, seducing individuals into spending time and money they can't afford. The gamble, in this context, offers solace: an illusion of control, adventure, and at times, victory over life's otherwise unyielding challenges.

Consider the harried professional, overwhelmed by deadlines and expectations. The spinning roulette provides a hypnotic escape from mounting pressure. Or perhaps it's a retiree grappling with the loss of purpose post-career, drawn to the poker table seeking camaraderie and the familiar thrill of competition. In both scenarios, the act of gambling momentarily silences inner demons, replacing them with the external chaos of high stakes games, chips, and strategy.

But while gambling offers an emotional sanctuary, it's a fragile facade. The temporary relief masks deeper issues that remain unresolved. The escape can quickly spiral into addiction, as individuals become trapped in a cycle of seeking solace through gambling, only to find themselves deeper in despair when the game ends. The emotional refuge becomes a prison, with walls built from debts, broken relationships, and unfulfilled promises.

Research on emotional escape in gambling shows a pattern of reliance on the behavior to cope with negative emotions. Studies suggest that individuals with high levels of depression, anxiety, or stress are more prone to use gambling as a coping mechanism. Their narratives often reveal a poignant quest for an emotional reprieve, though unfortunately, this reprieve often morphs into an unhealthy dependency.

To address this complex intertwining of emotion and behavior, interventions often focus on understanding the root emotional needs driving the escape. In therapy, individuals are encouraged to confront their fears and anxieties outside the gambling environment, providing them with healthier coping strategies. Cognitive-behavioral therapy, for example, examines these patterns, helping participants recognize their triggers and develop resilience without reverting to gambling.

The role of mindfulness cannot be overlooked in breaking this cycle. Mindfulness practices invite individuals to engage fully with their present emotions without judgment, helping them to recognize and validate their feelings rather than seeking distractions. When practiced consistently, mindfulness builds emotional awareness, enabling people to meet their emotional needs in more constructive and fulfilling ways.

Moreover, stories of recovery often reflect a common theme: the eventual realization that the emotional void filled by gambling was an illusion. Through support groups and personal reflection, many begin to uncover the underlying emotional triggers that spurred their gambling habits and start rebuilding their lives around more sustainable supports like friendships, hobbies, and professional help.

Ultimately, understanding gambling as an emotional escape sheds light on a crucial aspect of addiction. It underscores the importance of empathy, both in treating those who suffer from gambling addiction and in supporting them as they navigate the rocky path to recovery.

Emotional escape through gambling is a powerful pull, but with the right support and strategies, individuals can find their way back to a place of balance and well-being. In doing so, they aren't merely escaping; they are, in fact, courageously confronting life's complexity and embracing the journey to recovery with renewed hope.

Identifying Emotional Triggers

When exploring the emotional void that gambling seeks to fill, it becomes crucial to identify the emotional triggers that often drive individuals toward this behavior. Recognizing these triggers is a complex task, as emotions are deeply personal and can vary significantly from one individual to another. However, certain patterns and commonalities can provide a framework for understanding the emotional landscape of gambling addiction.

At its core, an emotional trigger is a stimulus that elicits a strong emotional response, often leading to a compulsion or urge. For many who gamble, these triggers may stem from feelings of anxiety, depression, or loneliness. The act of gambling temporarily alleviates these painful emotions by providing a sense of thrill, control, or escape. However, this relief is fleeting, often leading to a cyclical pattern where the emotional void only deepens, and the need to gamble grows more urgent.

Consider the experience of isolation, which is increasingly common in today's fast-paced, digitally connected world. Many individuals may find themselves feeling disconnected from others, leading to a profound sense of loneliness. In such cases, gambling becomes a substitute for the social interactions that are missing from their lives. The bustling environment of a casino or the competitive nature of online gaming communities can mimic a sense of belonging, albeit temporarily.

Stress is another potent emotional trigger. The pressures of modern life, including work, family responsibilities, and financial burdens, often leave individuals feeling overwhelmed. Gambling can present itself as an attractive avenue for stress relief. The focus required in placing bets or choosing numbers provides a distraction from real-world worries. Yet, the irony is that this escapism often generates additional stress, especially when financial loss occurs, perpetuating a vicious cycle.

On the other end of the spectrum, emotional highs can also act as triggers. For some, the excitement of a big win or the adrenaline rush of high-stakes betting serves as a catalyst for continued gambling. This phenomenon is closely tied to the brain's reward system, which seeks to replicate the conditions that produced such euphoria. Unfortunately, the pursuit of these emotional peaks can lead to reckless gambling behaviors and subsequent negative consequences.

It is essential to recognize that these emotions don't operate in isolation. Often, they interact with underlying psychological conditions, such as depression or anxiety disorders, amplifying their impact. Co-occurring mental health issues can exacerbate the feelings of despair or excitement that propel an individual towards gambling, making treatment and recovery more challenging.

Further complicating this emotional landscape are past experiences and traumas, which can have a lasting influence on one's relationship with gambling. Individuals with a history of trauma may turn to gambling as a means to cope with unresolved emotions and memories. The seductive nature of gambling's rewards can offer a temporary reprieve from painful past experiences, creating an emotional dependency.

To effectively identify and understand these emotional triggers, introspection and professional guidance may be necessary. Individuals often need to delve into their personal histories and emotional responses to uncover the roots of their gambling behaviors. Therapy and counseling can play a vital role in this process, helping individuals to not only recognize their triggers but also develop healthier coping mechanisms.

Through therapeutic interventions, individuals can learn to manage their emotions more effectively, reducing the power of these triggers. Cognitive Behavioral Therapy (CBT) is particularly effective in this regard, as it focuses on identifying and reshaping negative thought patterns and behaviors. By addressing the cognitive distortions associated with their emotional responses, individuals can gradually weaken the grip of gambling addiction.

Additionally, support groups and peer networks offer a communal space for individuals to share their experiences and learn from one another. The empathy and understanding gained in these environments can provide invaluable support, helping individuals to feel less isolated in their struggles and more empowered to confront their emotional triggers.

Understanding emotional triggers is not just about avoiding them but about cultivating resilience. Building emotional resilience involves developing strategies to handle stress, processing trauma, and rebuilding social connections. By enhancing resilience, individuals are better equipped to face their triggers without resorting to gambling as a coping mechanism.

Ultimately, the journey to understanding and overcoming emotional triggers is deeply personal and often challenging. Yet, with the right support and strategies, it is possible to reclaim one's life from the depths of the emotional void that gambling seeks to fill. Recognizing triggers is the first step on this path, paving the way towards recovery and a brighter, more fulfilling future.

Chapter 7:
Cultural Perspectives on Gambling

Gambling, a complex phenomenon, evolves within its cultural milieu, reflective of social values and historical narratives. Across diverse societies, from ancient civilizations that embraced dice games to modern-day states with bustling casinos, gambling reveals its multifaceted cultural dimensions. Cultural norms greatly influence gambling's acceptability, dictating not just practices but also the stigmas or esteem associated with it. In some cultures, it symbolizes wealth and social status, while in others it remains a clandestine activity shadowed by judgment. Looking closely, we see that rituals around gambling can embody cultural beliefs—fortune, fate, and luck interwoven with communal traditions. This interplay between culture and gambling extends beyond mere recreation; it affects societal attitudes towards risk and reward, shaping how communities perceive addiction. Understanding these cultural lenses is crucial in addressing gambling addiction, as it highlights the need for culturally sensitive approaches and interventions that respect the unique socio-cultural context of individuals grappling with this challenge.

Historical Contexts

The history of gambling is as rich and varied as the many cultures that have embraced it throughout the ages. From the earliest forms of betting found in ancient civilizations to the dazzling casinos of modern times, gambling has always held a mirror to human culture and its complexity. As we explore the historical contexts of gambling, it becomes clear that this activity is deeply woven into the fabric of societal development, driven by diverse motivations and evolving alongside humanity itself.

Ancient practices provide the first glimpse into humanity's fascination with wagers and games of chance. Archaeological findings suggest that gambling dates back at least to 3000 BCE when rudimentary dice, carved from sheep knuckles, were discovered in Mesopotamia. Similarly, the ancient Egyptians enjoyed a game known as "Senet," which some scholars believe involved elements of luck and strategy akin to gambling. These early examples reveal humanity's intrinsic draw to uncertainty and the suspense it brings.

The Greeks and Romans, whose histories brim with tales of gods and warriors, also indulged in games of chance. Greek mythology itself is rife with stories involving fate and fortune, illustrating an intertwined relationship between gambling and the philosophical concepts of destiny. The Romans, notorious for their love of public entertainment, frequently organized gambling events to amuse the masses. Both cultures legislated gambling practices, at times condemning them and, at others, espousing their virtues.

As we trace the evolution of gambling through the Middle Ages, we see it transformed by both legal and religious scrutiny. In Europe, card games emerged, spreading rapidly during the 15th century. Their popularity prompted regulatory measures, while simultaneously leading to the creation of prohibitions, often influenced by the Church's stance on moral conduct. This duality, where gambling represented both temptation and taboo, fueled its allure, setting the stage for its enduring presence in societal culture.

By the time we reach the 18th and 19th centuries, the Age of Enlightenment and the Industrial Revolution had profoundly impacted the perception of gambling. Lotteries became a popular means for governments to fund infrastructure without imposing new taxes, providing a socially acceptable veneer to what many considered a vice. In America, this period saw riverboat gambling thrive along the Mississippi; in Europe, opulent casinos began to pop up, becoming symbolic of affluence and sophistication.

The transformative power of gambling during the 20th century cannot be overstated. The legalization of casinos in Nevada in 1931 revolutionized the gambling landscape, birthing Las Vegas as the mecca of betting and chance. Meanwhile, the economic fluctuations brought about by the Great Depression and subsequent wars shaped gambling's role in society, as communities used it both as a source of escape and as a balm for economic woes.

During this period, gambling also began to reflect broader cultural shifts. The introduction of slot machines, for instance, made gambling more accessible and mechanical, removing some of the skill elements present in card games or horse betting. These changes characterized the modern evolution of gambling, reflecting a society increasingly comfortable with mechanization and instant gratification.

Gambling in the modern era has also been heavily influenced by globalization and technology. The rise of online gambling platforms in the late 20th and early 21st centuries marked a significant shift, marrying technology with tradition. This evolution reflects not only advancements in technology but also changes in societal attitudes towards accessibility and convenience in entertainment.

The historical contexts of gambling demonstrate a portrayal of human nature's multifaceted relationship with risk, reward, and recreation. It's a narrative of adaptability, reflecting societal changes and attitudes over time. Understanding these historical aspects helps contextualize modern gambling practices, offering insights into why certain games gain popularity and how societal perceptions influence legislative action.

In exploring the historical contexts of gambling, we recognize patterns and lessons that echo through time. These insights inform current attitudes towards betting activities, shaping public policy, informing psychological studies, and guiding effective intervention strategies. By understanding where gambling comes from, we can better address its modern challenges and manifestations, paving the way for a more nuanced and informed approach to its societal role.

Gambling Across Cultures

Gambling—a pastime that dances between chance and choice—is a global phenomenon embraced and shunned in equal measure across different cultures. Its cultural significance subtly shifts from one society to another, often revealing complex layers of values, traditions, and taboos. Whether nestled at a bustling Las Vegas casino or in a quiet Mahjong parlor in Beijing, gambling practices provide a mirror reflecting a society's relationship with risk, opportunity, and morality.

One of the most striking aspects of gambling across cultures is its historical footprint. Archaeological evidence suggests that rudimentary forms of gambling existed thousands of years ago. Ancient Chinese and Roman societies played games of chance, revealing early human fascination with risk and uncertainty. In some cultures, these games went beyond mere entertainment, becoming a part of religious ceremonies or social contracts, signifying trust and honor among participants.

The dichotomy of gambling as both a revered tradition and a frowned-upon vice is highlighted vividly in Asian cultures. In China, gambling is officially illegal except in Macau and Hong Kong. Yet, it pervades daily life, particularly during the Lunar New Year, when games of chance signify prosperity and luck. Conversely, in Japan, strict laws limit gambling, with exceptions like Pachinko, which skirts legality through loopholes. Here, gambling is woven tightly with cultural threads of honor and stoicism, yielding an experience distinct from Western norms.

In many Indigenous cultures, gambling holds ceremonial and social significance. For example, among Native American tribes, the practice has historical roots, often associated with storytelling and community gatherings. Today, the prevalence of tribal casinos reflects not only economic venture but also a complex interplay between tradition, autonomy, and modern enterprise.

European attitudes toward gambling vary considerably from country to country. The United Kingdom is home to a vibrant and regulated gambling industry, with its citizens participating enthusiastically in everything from sports betting to bingo. Here, gambling is often seen as a social activity, with deep roots in history. British pubs, once the venue for informal betting, now boast technological advancements facilitating gaming. On the flip side, countries like France impose stricter regulations and higher taxation, revealing a protective stance driven by societal concerns.

In the Middle East, where Islamic teachings strongly prohibit gambling, there are profound cultural implications tied to the practice. These restrictions are informed by religious doctrines that discourage any form of entity or action based solely on chance, often perceived as diverting from one's predictability by divine will. Despite such prohibitions, underground gambling rings exist, illustrating the universal allure of risk and reward despite legal and moral constraints.

Africa's gambling landscape is as diverse as its cultures. In countries like South Africa, the gambling sector is flourishing, driven by sports betting, particularly on football. On a broader scale, the continent faces the dual challenge of leveraging gambling as an economic booster while curbing potential addiction among impoverished populations. Here, cultural perspectives are heavily influenced by socio-economic factors, where gambling represents both opportunity and peril.

In Australia, gambling is ingrained in national culture to such an extent that it possesses one of the world's highest gambling rates per capita. From the Melbourne Cup, "the race that stops a nation," to thousands of Pokies machines in clubs, gambling is part of the social fabric.

This prevalence embodies a dual narrative: on one hand, it boosts the economy and on the other, it triggers ethical debates on its societal impact. The Australian approach reflects a broader cultural acceptance intertwined with the ongoing implications of addiction.

Globally, the digital revolution has further transformed gambling's cultural landscape. Online platforms transcend geographical and cultural barriers, offering a virtual arena for diverse betting experiences. Whether online poker, e-sports betting, or virtual casinos, technology allows for an unprecedented level of accessibility, challenging traditional cultural norms surrounding gambling.

Emergent technologies have sparked a cultural shift towards acceptance in regions where gambling was once taboo. Meanwhile, they serve as a catalyst for scrutiny and regulatory debates in areas with established gambling traditions. As technology continues to evolve, cultural perspectives on gambling will likely shift, reflecting broader changes in societal values and technological advancements.

Cultural variations also emerge in how societies address gambling addiction and recovery. In some regions, stigma deters individuals from seeking help, viewing addiction as a moral failing rather than a mental health issue. Conversely, other cultures adopt holistic approaches that incorporate traditional healing methods alongside contemporary therapies, underscoring the importance of cultural sensitivity in treatment practices.

The diverse cultural landscapes of gambling provide rich terrain for understanding addiction's psychological triggers. Each cultural context offers unique insights into why people gamble—whether for excitement, social bonding, or the allure of escaping economic hardship. These cultural narratives contribute to a broader understanding of gambling addiction, emphasizing the need for culturally tailored prevention and intervention strategies.

In conclusion, gambling serves as a lens through which various cultural identities and values are refracted. As societies continue to navigate the complex interplay of tradition, modernity, and morality, the cultural dimensions of gambling offer essential insights into the universal human experience of risk and reward. Each society's approach reveals a mosaic of beliefs and practices that together shape our global understanding of gambling and its profound psychological impact.

Chapter 8:
The Role of Technology

Technology's swift evolution has reshaped many aspects of modern life, and gambling is no exception. The convenience and accessibility offered by online platforms and mobile apps have dramatically increased the reach of gambling activities, often rendering them just a click away. This newfound accessibility can exacerbate gambling addiction by enabling continuous engagement, void of time or geographical constraints. With cleverly designed interfaces and immersive graphics, these digital environments often mimic the alluring atmosphere of physical casinos, but with greater intensity and personalization. Additionally, technology facilitates data collection, allowing operators to tailor experiences that maximize user engagement. Understanding these dynamics is crucial for addressing the psychological triggers that technology can amplify, which in turn can inform effective prevention and treatment strategies tailored to this digital era of gambling.

Online Gambling's Impact

In recent years, the landscape of gambling has undergone seismic shifts, primarily due to the digital revolution. Online gambling, heralded by many as a convenient pastime, has intricately woven itself into the tapestry of modern life. This shift has not only broadened access but also amplified the potential for addiction, altering the way individuals engage with gambling.

Online platforms thrive on accessibility. With just a smartphone, people can engage in gambling activities from virtually anywhere, anytime. This round-the-clock access removes physical barriers that once served as natural deterrents. For some, this convenience can swiftly spiral into compulsion, where boundaries blur, and control becomes elusive. The impacts of this unfettered access are profound, especially for those already teetering on the edge of addiction.

The digital interface itself significantly contributes to the addictive nature of online gambling. Bright graphics, engaging sound effects, and sophisticated algorithms are meticulously crafted to capture attention and enhance the user experience. These elements stimulate the brain's reward system, releasing dopamine and creating a cycle of anticipation and gratification that can be incredibly hard to break.

Furthermore, many online gambling platforms employ sophisticated reinforcement schedules designed to keep users engaged. Small, frequent wins are often interspersed with the lure of a larger jackpot, ensuring players remain hopeful and invested. This tactic mirrors the same psychological hooks found in traditional gaming but with added intensity due to the platform's immersive nature.

Social elements also play a decisive role in online gambling's impact. Many platforms integrate features that mimic social network interactions, allowing players to compete with others or share their achievements. These dynamics can foster a false sense of community and connection, enticing users to stay longer and play more aggressively.

Moreover, online gambling is often accompanied by deceptive marketing strategies that obscure the risks involved. Advertisements portray it as an easy, glamorous way to win money, which can lead to unrealistic expectations. Individuals may not fully recognize the potential for loss or the odds stacked against them, creating a potent recipe for addiction and financial peril.

Youth and adolescents are particularly susceptible to the allure of online gambling. Growing up in a digital age, they are adept at navigating online platforms, but often lack the maturity to understand the repercussions of gambling. The gamification of these platforms can disguise gambling as harmless entertainment, making it easier for younger individuals to fall into addictive behaviors, sometimes before they're even legally allowed to gamble.

As online gambling becomes more entrenched in the digital economy, the risk of its normalization grows. It can mask the seriousness of compulsive gambling behaviors, as those afflicted may underestimate their problem simply because they're part of a larger, seemingly norm-driven trend. This normalization also complicates the identification and treatment of addiction, as the digital nature of the habit makes it less visible and consequently, less likely to be addressed in clinical settings.

Despite these risks, online gambling does offer certain advantages. With proper regulations and technological measures, it holds the potential to foster responsible gaming habits. For instance, limits on betting amounts and time spent can be more easily enforced online. Additionally, some platforms provide tools for self-exclusion and offer resources for individuals to seek help when needed.

The interplay between technology and gambling is complex and multifaceted, with each advancement presenting both opportunities for engagement and challenges in addiction control. As we continue to navigate this digital frontier, understanding the psychological underpinnings of online gambling becomes increasingly crucial. This insight informs strategies aimed at minimizing harm and fostering a healthier relationship with gambling.

The ultimate impact of online gambling will likely be determined by how society chooses to address and manage these challenges. Through informed policymaking, education, and the development of supportive communities, it is possible to strike a balance that enables enjoyment without falling into the pitfalls of addiction.

As we assess the reach of online gambling, it becomes evident that technology's role in the gambling landscape is as influential as it is inevitable. The question remains: how can we harness this technology to empower individuals, rather than ensnare them in the cycle of addiction? The answer lies in transforming awareness into action, crafting a future where technology aids in recovery and resilience.

The Rise of Mobile Betting

The landscape of gambling has been significantly reshaped by the advent of mobile technology. Unlike traditional gambling venues, mobile betting offers a new level of accessibility and convenience that is hard to ignore. It's no longer necessary for individuals to travel to a casino or racetrack; now, they can easily place bets from virtually anywhere using their smartphones. This shift has profound implications for the gambling industry, for those who gamble, and importantly, for understanding gambling addiction.

Mobile betting's rapid rise is linked to the ubiquity of smartphones. These devices have become an indispensable part of modern life, putting casino-like experiences into the hands of millions worldwide. As this technology continues to evolve, the barrier for entry into the world of gambling lowers. For some, this results in recreational entertainment; for others, it can mean the beginning of compulsive habits that are difficult to control. Understanding this dynamic is crucial in identifying the psychological mechanisms that contribute to addiction.

One of the most striking features of mobile betting is its capacity for personalization. Advanced algorithms allow betting apps to tailor suggestions and prompts based on individual user behavior. This customization heightens engagement, creating an environment where choices feel uniquely personal, yet subtly manipulated. The persuasive design of mobile interfaces mimics social media strategies: notifications, streaks, and quick rewards. This fosters a cycle of anticipation and gratification, elements known to strengthen addictive behavior.

Consider the sheer variety of gambling options now available at one's fingertips. Whether it's sports betting, virtual casinos, or fantasy leagues, mobile betting platforms are diverse and multifaceted. This variety not only attracts a wide audience but also facilitates continuous engagement. Bettors can switch between games with a swipe, experiencing constant novelty without interruption. Such seamless transitions between different forms of gambling can blur the line between casual play and addiction.

Financial transactions via mobile betting have also become incredibly streamlined. Modern platforms offer in-app purchases and digital wallets, simplifying the process of depositing and withdrawing money. This ease can desensitize users to the real value of money, leading them to spend more than they might in a physical setting. Furthermore, quick and easy transfers contribute to the illusion of inconsequential stakes, which encourages riskier betting behavior.

Detachment from reality is another psychological component enabled by mobile betting. The digital environment creates a sense of anonymity and privacy, allowing individuals to engage in gambling behaviors they might avoid in a social context. This absence of social scrutiny can be especially detrimental for those already vulnerable to addictive behaviors. The sensation of playing in an insular world can distort risk perception, leading to decisions that wouldn't be made face-to-face with a dealer or fellow player.

Moreover, the pervasive presence of smartphones means there's constant exposure to gambling opportunities. Push notifications and personalized marketing efforts ensure that the temptation to bet is always just a swipe away. This persistent accessibility prevents the kind of breaks that might naturally occur with more traditional forms of gambling. The lack of downtime can exacerbate impulses and reduce the chance for critical reflection or restraint.

While mobile technology offers alluring convenience for users, it also presents a significant challenge for those seeking to regulate gambling habits or assist individuals in recovery. The very features that make mobile betting appealing are also those that can make it compulsive. For mental health professionals and addiction treatment specialists, finding effective intervention strategies requires a deep understanding of these technological influences and how they intersect with psychological vulnerabilities.

To address the challenges posed by mobile betting, it's important to develop tools that can help individuals monitor and control their gambling behavior. One potential solution is the implementation of time and spending limits within the apps themselves. Some platforms have begun to integrate features that allow users to set self-imposed restrictions, offering a form of self-regulation. However, these measures rely heavily on the individual's commitment and awareness.

Parental controls and digital literacy programs are another avenue for addressing the risks associated with mobile betting. Educating young people about the potential dangers before they even encounter these apps can provide a buffer against developing harmful habits. Since youths are particularly susceptible to online influences due to their high engagement with technology, early intervention can be a particularly effective prevention strategy.

From an ethical standpoint, the responsibility for mitigating the risks of mobile betting doesn't just fall on users. The companies behind these platforms must also play a role in promoting healthier gambling environments. This includes being transparent about the algorithms used for personalization and being proactive in flagging signs of problematic behavior. The integration of AI and machine learning could aid in developing predictive tools that identify at-risk users and provide timely support.

In conclusion, the rise of mobile betting represents a significant evolution in the gambling landscape, posing unique challenges and opportunities in understanding gambling addiction. While the draw of convenience and personalization is undeniable, it's crucial to address the psychological and technological forces that can transform leisurely gambling into compulsive behavior. A collaborative approach involving users, developers, and researchers can pave the way toward healthier engagement with this evolving frontier.

Chapter 9:
Social Influences

Social influences weave an intricate pattern in the tapestry of gambling addiction, often guiding individuals down paths they might not have chosen on their own. The subtle power of peer pressure and family dynamics can ignite the first sparks of gambling interest, amplifying the allure of the game with whispers of acceptance and belonging. Friends might innocently coax one to place a bet, marking the genesis of a habit that can spiral into dependency. Simultaneously, family environments play a dual-edged role; they can either nurture resilience against or inadvertently perpetuate the cycle of addiction through modeling behaviors and unspoken expectations. Within these frameworks, gambling becomes a shared experience laden with emotional ties, complicating efforts to break free. Understanding these social currents is crucial in unraveling the complex motives behind gambling, offering insight into targeted prevention and intervention strategies that address these influential relationships.

Peer Pressure and Gambling

Peer pressure, often associated with adolescence, reaches far beyond school hallways and neighborhood parks. In the realm of gambling, it becomes a significant social catalyst that can lead individuals down the path of addiction. The need to fit in and gain acceptance from peers can be an incredibly powerful motivator, sometimes driving people to engage in risky behaviors they might not otherwise consider.

In social settings, gambling is frequently touted as a communal activity — something done with friends, family, or colleagues. This communal aspect can blur the lines between harmless fun and compulsive behavior. When in a group, individuals may feel compelled to place bets, join games, or enter casinos, echoing the choices of those around them. This dynamic is particularly influential when the group comprises avid gamblers who glorify the lifestyle and minimize its dangers.

For those susceptible to peer pressure, the social environment can significantly alter perceptions of gambling risk. The excitement and acceptance from peers might overshadow the recognition of gambling's dangers. This dynamic becomes more concerning with the portrayal of success stories at the poker table or slot machines, which can make the allure of gambling seem overwhelmingly positive while glossing over the potential for significant loss.

Peer pressure doesn't just manifest in direct invitations or coercive statements. Often, it is subtle, brought on by feelings of exclusion. Watching friends partake in gambling activities can evoke the fear of missing out (commonly known as FOMO), triggering a compulsion to participate, not from personal interest, but from a desire for inclusion. These experiences can be particularly overwhelming for individuals who lack confidence or who already struggle with self-esteem issues.

Interestingly, the influence of peer pressure can vary across different age groups. Young adults, who are navigating identity formation, may be particularly vulnerable. They are often eager to establish social networks and are prone to engage in whatever activities their chosen peer groups deem acceptable, including gambling. This vulnerable stage is a breeding ground for problematic behavior, as the brain's executive processes for decision-making and risk assessment are still developing.

However, it would be a mistake to conclude that only young people are swayed by peer pressure. Adults, too, are not immune. Professional environments that encourage gambling as a form of networking — like poker nights or fantasy sports leagues — can create an atmosphere where participation feels necessary for career advancement or social standing. In such cases, refusing to participate might seem like opting out of broader career or social opportunities.

Social media adds yet another layer to this issue. Platforms like Facebook, Instagram, and TikTok offer countless examples of people celebrating their gambling wins. This online portrayal creates an illusion of normalcy and success in gambling, rarely discussing the reality of losses. The 'highlight reel' nature of social media induces peer pressure at scale, fostering a virtual environment where everyone appears to be winning, and thus, subtly encouraging participation.

Recognizing peer pressure as a factor in gambling addiction requires understanding some psychological principles. Social identity theory, for instance, underlines the importance of group membership in shaping behavior. People often emulate the behaviors and attitudes of their desired social group. When such groups indulge in gambling, the behavioral norms shift, encouraging others to partake in the same activities to maintain group cohesion and support.

Overcoming the effects of peer pressure in gambling requires a multifaceted approach. Education on the risks and realities of gambling can empower individuals to make informed decisions rather than reactive ones. Social campaigns that highlight both the potential harms of gambling and the power of resisting peer influence can reshape perceptions and encourage healthier choices.

Support networks play a crucial role in counteracting negative peer influences. Cultivating friendships with individuals who value activities that don't involve gambling can create a new normal where the pressure to gamble diminishes. These positive influences can be a lifeline for those struggling to break free from the cycle of gambling prompted by peers.

Engaging in open conversations about gambling addiction and its triggers is essential in mitigating the effects of peer pressure. Friends and family members who are aware of their loved one's gambling issues can serve as allies, providing encouragement and understanding while promoting alternative social activities. Such open dialogue reduces the stigma around refusing to gamble, making it easier for individuals to resist peer pressure.

In terms of prevention and intervention, strategies designed to build resilience against peer pressure are crucial. Programs that focus on enhancing self-esteem, decision-making skills, and assertiveness can equip individuals with the tools needed to resist peer pressure effectively. These programs are particularly crucial in environments prone to high peer influence, such as schools, colleges, and workplaces.

Ultimately, understanding the role of peer pressure in gambling addiction illuminates a path toward prevention and recovery. By fostering environments that emphasize informed choice and individual agency, society can mitigate the damaging effects of peer influence. Addressing peer pressure is not just about saying "no" to gambling — it's about empowering individuals to choose the path that aligns with their values, irrespective of external pressures.

Family Dynamics

Family dynamics play a crucial role in shaping individual behavior patterns, particularly when it comes to gambling addiction. The family environment can act as a powerful social influence, either mitigating or exacerbating the predisposition towards gambling. Within the familial context, relationships are complex and multifaceted, interacting through a web of emotional and social exchanges. These interactions can inadvertently become catalysts for addictive behaviors, like gambling.

Families serve as the initial social units where individuals learn behaviors, form attitudes, and adopt coping mechanisms. Unfortunately, dysfunctional family dynamics can lead to maladaptive coping behaviors such as gambling. For instance, children growing up in households where gambling is normalized or even idealized may view it as a harmless or routine form of entertainment. When family members model risky behaviors or have a dismissive attitude towards gambling, they can unintentionally encourage similar patterns in younger generations.

Communication—or the lack of it—within families also plays a significant role in gambling behavior. Open, honest dialogue can be a deterrent to gambling addiction by providing a supportive environment where individuals can express their struggles without fear of judgment. Conversely, families that shy away from these discussions may inadvertently push individuals towards gambling as a coping mechanism for unexpressed emotions or conflicts.

The emotional fabric of a family can be a double-edged sword. Acts of love and concern can create a safety net, helping prevent gambling problems from escalating. Yet, these same emotions can produce enabling behaviors. For instance, a family may cover up financial losses to protect a loved one, unknowingly perpetuating the cycle of addiction. The desire to shield family members from consequences might come from a place of love but often serves to delay necessary interventions.

Parental influence, both overt and subtle, leaves a lasting impact. Children who witness gambling as a frequent activity within the household are likely to perceive it as a normal aspect of recreation. Further, parents' attitudes toward risk-taking and financial irresponsibility might unconsciously seep into their children's psyche, paving the way for similar tendencies.

Siblings, too, can exert influence. The dynamics between siblings—ranging from rivalry to camaraderie—might play a role in one's inclination to gamble. For instance, in some cases, a younger sibling might mimic the behaviors of an older sibling they admire, including gambling habits. Alternatively, competition among siblings could lead to gambling as a form of one-upmanship.

Another aspect to consider is the socio-economic status of the family, which often dictates attitudes toward money and risk. In families with financial instability, gambling can be wrongly perceived as a quick fix for money woes. This perception, over time, can take root and evolve into a full-fledged addiction, perpetuated by false hope and desperation.

Interestingly, cultural norms embedded within a family can also contribute significantly. In certain cultures or communities where gambling is part of tradition or social gatherings, individuals are more likely to view it as an acceptable pastime. This cultural acceptance, deeply ingrained in family traditions, can make it difficult to identify gambling behavior as problematic until it's too late.

Emotional neglect within families creates another breeding ground for gambling addiction. Individuals who don't receive adequate emotional support, love, and attention may seek these feelings elsewhere. Gambling can become a surrogate for the missing emotional connection, offering a temporary, albeit unhealthy, escape from reality.

This interaction between family dynamics and gambling behavior is not a one-way street. The repercussions of a family member's gambling addiction can ripple through the household, affecting relationships and the mental health of other members. Trust can break down, and financial stress can mount, leading to a vicious cycle that can perpetuate addiction.

The role of family support systems in recovery cannot be overstated. Families that understand the nuances of addiction, engage in supportive dialogues, and create an empathetic environment can drastically influence positive outcomes. This involves acknowledging the addiction's impact on the family and striving for collective healing, which is often a critical component of treatment and recovery.

In summary, the influence of family dynamics on gambling behavior is profound and multifaceted. The family unit, through its complexities, has the potential to both nurture and deter gambling addiction. Understanding these intricate dynamics can aid in developing comprehensive strategies for prevention and intervention, ensuring that individuals are supported in overcoming their addictive behaviors.

Chapter 10:
Financial Implications

In the shadowy world of gambling addiction, the financial implications can be as destructive as the emotional and psychological ones. When the thrill transforms into desperation, mounting debts become a silent companion, perpetuating a cycle that often spirals into financial ruin. The allure of retrieving what has been lost can lead individuals down a path of risky financial behavior, creating a ripple effect that disrupts families and communities. The economic impact extends beyond personal loss, touching societal levels as healthcare and legal systems strain under the burden of supporting those grappling with the ramifications of their addiction. Financial recovery isn't just about balancing checkbooks or paying off creditors; it's about reconstructing lives and restoring hope. By understanding these profound impacts, we pave the way towards meaningful interventions and the development of comprehensive support systems that address both the psychological and fiscal tolls of gambling addiction.

Debt and Desperation

Staring at the insurmountable pile of bills, a person might wonder how innocent indulgence spiraled into such severe financial strain. The issue at hand isn't simply a collection of unpaid debts; it's a tale of desperation that paints the backdrop of many lives entrapped by gambling addiction. As gambling becomes more than just a recreational activity, it morphs into a relentless chase for financial relief—a chase where the stakes are ever-increasing and the outcomes are devastating.

Often, the road to crippling debt begins quietly. A series of small losses may seem manageable at first, a mere hiccup in one's financial life. But as losses accumulate, the instinctual drive is to recoup them, to make sense of the sunk costs by "winning it all back." This notion of overturning bad luck fosters a cycle of increasing wagers and risky bets. Ironically, the attempt to solve financial problems through additional gambling often deepens the hole, transforming a troubling habit into an all-consuming necessity.

The desperation fueled by burgeoning debt extends beyond the financial sphere; it becomes a psychological ordeal. There's an emotional seesaw between hope and hopelessness, galvanized by each spin of the wheel or turn of the card. When hope makes way for despair, many individuals find themselves ensnared in a web of secrecy, driven by guilt and fear of judgment. The social facade remains intact while the foundational supports of one's life erode silently.

This secrecy can foster isolation and heighten stress. The individual's social circle begins to thin as debts stack up and the fear of exposure grows. Friends and family may notice changes, but the individual, gripped by the lure of restoring financial stability through gambling, often isolates themselves further. This isolation is a breeding ground for desperation—it creates an echo chamber where the only voice that resonates is that of the desperate gambler, promising that one big win will fix everything.

Financial desperation can also lead to unethical or illegal activities as individuals grapple with mounting pressure. Borrowing money becomes habitual—first from friends and then from creditors. It's not uncommon for someone in the throes of desperation to resort to high-interest loans or even deception to procure funds. This brings about not only financial ruin but also legal ramifications, adding another layer to the pile of consequences waiting at the gambler's doorstep.

Moreover, the emotional stress of debt can spill over into other areas of life, significantly affecting mental health. Anxiety and depression are common companions, ushered in by the relentless demands of unpaid bills and creditors, compounding the sense of despair. This mental anguish can cloud judgment, further binding the individual to the cycle of betting and losing. In attempting to alleviate financial crises through gambling, the emotional cost can become as debilitating as the financial one.

The intersection of debt and desperation serves as a critical turning point. It is often when many individuals seek help, realizing that the situation has become untenable on their own. Yet, it is a situation marred by the difficulty of breaking emotional and psychological ties to gambling. For some, witnessing the extent of their financial downfall is the crucial wake-up call to pursue change and seek avenues of recovery.

In helplines and therapy rooms, stories of financial woes are told and retold, echoing with the common thread of desperation's financial toll. Recovery begins with understanding, where one must confront the stark realities of their circumstances, recognizing that change is the only path toward resolution. Financial counseling, alongside psychological intervention, plays a crucial role here, offering a roadmap to rebuild fractured lives.

One story tells of an individual who, upon reaching the depths of financial despair, found a way to transform desperation into motivation. With guidance and support, they began unraveling the tangled web of debts they had woven, learning sustainable financial habits. This journey underscores the potential for change—that with structured support and determination, financial traps can eventually loosen their grip, allowing hope to replace desperation.

While financial recovery is fraught with challenges, it is essential to highlight the inspirational aspect of overcoming such adversity. For many, confronting the desperation tied to gambling debts reveals inner strength and resilience they never knew existed. In navigating the frustratingly slow path to financial recovery, individuals often discover a renewed sense of self-worth and discipline.

In conclusion, the story of debt and desperation is not an endpoint but rather a segment of a larger narrative. It illustrates the profundity of gambling addiction's impact not only on one's wallet but also on their psyche and interpersonal relationships. Understanding this facet is vital in moving forward, shedding light on the mechanisms that perpetuate the cycle of addiction and paving the way for healing and hope in the journeys of countless individuals seeking redemption and recovery.

Economic Impact of Addiction

In exploring the financial implications of gambling addiction, the economic impact stands as a profound pillar that underscores the gravity of this affliction. At both the individual and societal levels, gambling addiction doesn't merely drain personal finances; it disrupts entire communities and economies. Those entangled in gambling addiction often find themselves in a cycle of financial desperation, escalating debt, and potential economic ruin, while broader societal costs accrue in less overt yet significant ways.

For the individual, the economic impact of a gambling addiction is often felt sharply and painfully. Financial resources that could have been invested in personal growth, education, or family needs are instead funneled into a habit that echoes with diminishing returns. The persistent hope of recouping losses only deepens the financial chasm, often leading to considerable debt. This debt, fueled by a mix of denial and optimism, can lead to a cascade of economic consequences including loss of assets, poor credit ratings, and in extreme cases, bankruptcy. In many instances, the addicted gambler may resort to borrowing from friends, family, or even financial institutions, creating strained relationships and increasing financial liabilities.

The ramifications extend beyond the monetary losses on an individual level; they infiltrate close personal relationships. Household budgets collapse under the weight of uncontrolled gambling expenditures, leading to profound tension among family members. The stress of financial instability can cause fractures in marriages or partnerships, as trust is eroded by concealed debts and financial mismanagement. For children growing up in these environments, the knock-on effects can include a lack of educational opportunities and an unstable home life.

Beyond the walls of individual households, the economic impact spirals outward, affecting the workplace and, consequently, the broader economy. Research indicates that individuals suffering from gambling addiction often experience a decline in job performance. Absenteeism, distraction, and decreased productivity are not uncommon, potentially costing businesses significant sums in lost productivity. Moreover, gambling-related employment issues can sometimes lead to job loss, adding to the economic burden on both the individual and society.

It's not just businesses that bear the brunt of gambling addiction; governments face economic pressures as well. Resources are diverted to provide support services, treatment programs, and counseling for those affected. In some cases, the legal system becomes involved, further straining public resources. The need for extensive social services can cause increased taxation and redistribution of funds that could be directed toward other public goods or necessary infrastructure. Governments also contend with the challenge of balancing the economic benefits derived from casino taxes and related revenues with the social costs of gambling addiction. It's a delicate equilibrium, fraught with moral and economic dilemmas.

The public health aspect of gambling addiction also brings notable economic considerations. Healthcare costs surge as individuals struggling with addiction require medical attention for related mental health issues, such as anxiety and depression. There are also indirect costs to health systems through stress-related illnesses that arise in individuals closely impacted by the gambler's activities, further amplifying the economic strain on health services providers and public health budgets.

Moreover, the community at large faces more subtle but pervasive economic setbacks. Neighborhood crime rates can rise as desperate individuals turn to illegal activities to fund their gambling habits, increasing community policing costs and judicial expenditures. This cascade of economic detriment erodes community welfare, leading to a decline in community resources and quality of life.

On a macroeconomic scale, gambling addiction can skew market dynamics, dampening consumer spending in healthier economic sectors. The funds funneled into gambling enterprises are often funds that could otherwise stimulate local economies through purchases in retail, dining, travel, and education. During economic analyses, such distortions reveal an underlying fragility in the financial ecosystem, where investment in social wellbeing and development takes a backseat to the immediate gratification provided by gambling.

The question of economic impact sparks a broader ethical debate about the responsibility of the gambling industry, alongside governmental accountability. Industry operators generate significant revenue streams, sometimes at the detriment of vulnerable populations. Discussions about responsible gaming, self-exclusion programs, and ethical advertising are rife with economic undertones as stakeholders balance profit with people.

The stark economic realities of gambling addiction demand a multifaceted approach to prevention and support. While blanket prohibitions aren't necessarily effective, they highlight the necessity for comprehensive educational campaigns, stringent regulation, and robust support frameworks. Building economic resilience in potential victims holds promise in reducing the devastating economic footprint of gambling addiction.

In conclusion, the economic impact of gambling addiction is extensive, interwoven with personal tragedies and larger societal consequences. The financial devastation witnessed by individuals often leads to deeper societal costs, necessitating robust intervention strategies. As we delve further into understanding the psychological triggers and mechanisms behind gambling addiction, we arm ourselves with the knowledge and empathy required to mitigate these economic blights, ensuring healthier economic futures both personally and communal-wise.

Chapter 11:
The Comorbidity Factor

Understanding the intricate connection between gambling addiction and other mental health issues is crucial for grasping the full extent of this challenging problem. Often, individuals struggling with gambling addiction face a tangled web of comorbid conditions, such as anxiety, depression, or substance abuse, which can complicate their path to recovery. These co-occurring disorders not only amplify the intensity of the addiction but also obscure the clarity needed for healing. By examining the interconnectedness of mental health and gambling, we can illuminate the underlying psychological complexities that drive compulsive behavior and identify more holistic approaches to treatment. Recognizing these connections equips professionals and those affected with the insights needed to address the root causes of addiction, fostering an environment where comprehensive recovery is possible. As we delve into this multifaceted relationship, it becomes clear that successful intervention must consider the entire spectrum of a person's mental health landscape, paving the way for more effective prevention and support strategies.

Mental Health and Gambling

In the intricate web of gambling addiction, mental health often plays a critical, yet sometimes overlooked, role. Gambling doesn't just exist as an isolated act of wagering money on uncertain outcomes; it intertwines deeply with the psychological fabric of an individual.

Comorbid mental health issues can exacerbate gambling tendencies and create a vicious cycle that is challenging to break. Individuals with existing mental health disorders frequently turn to gambling as a coping mechanism, further complicating their emotional and psychological landscape.

Many people with gambling addiction struggle with depression, anxiety, or other mood disorders. These conditions can enhance the appeal of gambling as a temporary escape from unfavorable emotional states. For a moment, the thrill of a potential win provides a respite from feelings of sadness or anxiety. However, this temporary relief can significantly deteriorate one's mental health over time. As losses accumulate, so do feelings of despair and hopelessness, reinforcing the initial depressive or anxious state.

Interestingly, the impulsive nature of gambling aligns with the symptoms of certain mental health disorders. Impulse control disorders, such as ADHD, often co-occur with gambling addiction. The impulsivity associated with ADHD can lead individuals to make hasty decisions, ignore potential consequences, and continuously engage in risky betting behavior. Moreover, gambling itself may aggravate underlying impulsivity, creating a feedback loop that's hard to escape from.

Bipolar disorder is another mental health condition that can intertwine with gambling behavior. During manic phases, an individual might be drawn to the thrill of high-stakes gambling, fueled by excessive confidence and a diminished perception of risk. These manic episodes can lead to severe financial consequences that can trigger depressive episodes, thus spiraling into further gambling as a means of escape. The emotional highs and lows of both gambling and bipolar disorder can be doubly destructive when they interact, creating emotional turbulence and financial instability.

The nuanced connection between mental health and gambling also extends to social anxiety disorder. For individuals with social anxiety, gambling, particularly online gambling, offers an enticing avenue for social interaction without the pressure of direct human contact. The anonymity of online platforms provides a sense of safety, yet it can also result in prolonged periods of gambling, which only serves to further isolate the individual.

It's crucial for mental health professionals to view gambling addiction through a multifaceted lens. By understanding the underlying mental health conditions that may coexist with gambling issues, clinicians can better tailor treatment approaches. Cognitive Behavioral Therapy (CBT), for instance, can be highly effective not only for addressing compulsive gambling but also for tackling co-occurring disorders like depression or anxiety. This integrated approach is vital in breaking the cycle of comorbidity.

Additionally, therapeutic interventions should focus on building resilience and developing healthier coping mechanisms. Teaching individuals to recognize their emotional triggers and equipping them with tools to manage these emotions without resorting to gambling is key. Mindfulness practices and stress-reduction techniques can serve as valuable strategies in both individual and group therapy settings.

Stigma surrounding both gambling addiction and mental health can often deter individuals from seeking help. The fear of judgment or societal perception that primarily associates gambling behavior with lack of self-control can prevent open discussion about mental health struggles. Providing education and increasing awareness can help to break down these barriers, encouraging those affected to seek support and understanding.

Advocacy for mental health care as a component of gambling addiction treatment is essential. With increased recognition of the comorbid relationship between mental health and gambling, both public health policies and individual treatment plans can evolve. Ensuring access to mental health services for those battling gambling addiction can make a profound difference in recovery trajectories.

In conclusion, the relationship between mental health and gambling is complex and requires a nuanced approach to understanding and treatment. By acknowledging the role of mental health disorders in the development and perpetuation of gambling addiction, a holistic approach to care can be developed. This means not only addressing the gambling behavior but also seeking to heal the mind's underlying wounds, thereby offering a clearer path to recovery.

Substance Abuse Connections

Substance abuse and gambling addiction often walk hand in hand, forming a complex web of psychological dependencies. As we delve into the association between these seemingly disparate issues, it becomes apparent that they share more than just underlying vulnerabilities. Both can emerge from the same dark corners of human emotion and cognition, driven by similar psychological forces and neurological pathways. Understanding this connection is crucial for both mitigating risk and devising effective treatment strategies.

At the core, both substance abuse and gambling addiction interact with the brain's reward system in a highly compelling manner. The intoxicating high of winning a bet mirrors the chemical rush of alcohol or drugs, rooted in the surges of dopamine—a key neurotransmitter responsible for feelings of pleasure and satisfaction. When a person gambles or uses substances, this dopamine release creates a reinforcing cycle, making them chase that initial euphoria. This biochemical feedback loop often spirals into compulsive behavior, where the individual loses control over their activities.

The overlap between gambling and substance abuse isn't limited to biochemical mechanisms. Psychological factors play a huge role as well. Stress, trauma, depression, and anxiety are common triggers for both behaviors. Many individuals use gambling and substances as means to escape from emotional pain or unresolved issues. This form of self-medication can provide temporary relief, but it may lead to long-term harm, as the root causes remain unaddressed and the dependency grows stronger.

Moreover, the social environments that foster gambling and substance abuse can be quite similar. Peer influence, family dynamics, and social settings often nurture or trigger these behaviors. A person surrounded by family members who gamble or consume substances is more likely to engage in similar activities. In some cases, the societal acceptance—or even glamorization—of both activities further entices individuals to indulge, ignoring the potential consequences.

It's important to consider the demographic overlap as well. Studies have consistently shown that individuals with gambling problems are more likely to also have substance use disorders. This dual diagnosis is not just coincidence but highlights the intertwined nature of these addictions. The presence of one addictive disorder significantly increases the probability of the other, potentially due to shared genetic, environmental, and psychological factors.

From an epidemiological perspective, identifying individuals at risk of both gambling addiction and substance abuse can be challenging. Yet, it is vital for prevention efforts. Screening for gambling behaviors in substance use treatment programs—or vice versa—can be a starting point. This integrated approach enables early identification and treatment of co-occurring disorders, which is often essential for successful recovery.

Furthermore, the treatment strategies for these comorbid disorders need to be tailored, taking into account the unique interplay between them. Traditional substance abuse intervention methods may not be wholly effective unless they address the gambling component, and the same holds true in reverse. Cognitive Behavioral Therapy (CBT) and motivational interviewing are commonly employed techniques, as they help reshape the detrimental thought patterns and improve motivation towards recovery.

Support systems also play a crucial role in recovery for individuals dealing with both substance abuse and gambling issues. Group therapies provide a shared space where experiences can be exchanged, and mutual support can be harnessed. Likewise, family involvement is key. Educating loved ones on the nuances of dual disorders fosters empathy and understanding, giving patients better support networks to lean on during their recovery journeys.

Lastly, research into these interconnected phenomena is ongoing, aiming to uncover more about how these addictions develop and interact. As science advances, new insights and technological innovations hold the promise of better predictive tools which can identify individuals at risk more accurately and provide them with early intervention options. The future of tackling these intertwined challenges looks hopeful, with a focus on comprehensive, individualized care that addresses both gambling addiction and substance abuse simultaneously.

In summary, the link between substance abuse and gambling addiction is complex yet significant. Recognizing their shared foundations allows us to approach treatment in a more holistic and effective manner. Addressing both disorders together fosters a more robust pathway to recovery, reducing the likelihood of relapse and supporting the individual's journey towards a healthier life. With continued research and awareness, society can improve prevention strategies, offering hope to those caught in the cycle of addiction.

Chapter 12:
Gender Differences

In exploring the intricate landscape of gambling addiction, it's crucial to understand that gender plays a pivotal role in how individuals experience and engage with gambling behaviors. Men and women often gravitate towards different forms of gambling which can be traced back to societal expectations and traditional gender roles. Men frequently display a tendency towards competitive and strategic gambling activities such as poker or sports betting, driven by a societal narrative that valorizes risk-taking. In contrast, women may be more inclined toward games of chance like slot machines and bingo, which are sometimes pursued as a means of emotional escape or socialization rather than competition. These differences are not just cultural artifacts but are intertwined with psychological and emotional motivations unique to each gender. Recognizing these differences is vital for developing effective prevention and treatment strategies that are sensitive to the unique needs and triggers experienced by men and women in the realm of gambling addiction.

How Men and Women Gamble Differently

Throughout history, gambling has served as a tempting arena where individuals test their luck and will. Yet, hidden beneath the glares of casino lights and the flickering of slot machines, a profound divide exists in how men and women experience this allure. The intersection of psychology, biology, and societal norms crafts distinct pathways for male and female gambling behaviors. Understanding these pathways not only broadens our comprehension of gambling addiction but also contributes to tailoring more effective prevention and recovery strategies.

An intriguing aspect of gambling behavior that merits attention is the differing motivations that drive men and women. Men often gamble for the thrill and competitiveness associated with the activity. They are drawn to games of skill where the possibility of dominating an opponent offers a tantalizing rush. In contrast, women are more likely to engage in gambling as a form of escape from emotional stress or as a means of social interaction. Games that offer a social component, like bingo or slot machines, are particularly appealing to women, providing a break from daily pressures in a seemingly controlled environment.

These differing motivations are underscored by divergent patterns of gambling preferences. Men typically prefer strategic games such as poker or sports betting, where personal skill is perceived to influence the outcome. This preference aligns with cultural expectations of masculinity, emphasizing control and mastery over chance. On the other hand, women often gravitate towards games with fixed-odds such as lottery or slot machines. These games are considered more luck-based, aligning with how femininity has historically been associated with passivity and fortune.

Delving further into the psychology, the social and emotional connections that women seek through gambling often serve as both a coping mechanism and a driver of addiction. This social aspect can be viewed through two lenses: community and isolation. While some women find pleasure in the communal experiences that gambling provides, it can simultaneously act as a vehicle for solitude, offering an intimate retreat where they feel unjudged and capable of navigating their emotions in private. However, this retreat can quickly transform into a vicious cycle, where the emotional refuge becomes a binding dependency.

Moreover, biological differences also play a role in how men and women gamble differently. Research suggests that women generally experience a stronger emotional response to gambling wins and losses compared to men. This heightened emotional sensitivity can potentially accelerate the trajectory from casual participation to problematic gambling behaviors. Additionally, studies indicate variations in dopamine release between genders, a chemical critical to the brain's reward system, further shaping the addiction pathway.

Societal norms and expectations further exacerbate these differences. Traditional gender roles, which are entrenched in society, dictate the way men and women are 'allowed' to indulge in or express their gambling habits. Men are often socially encouraged to partake in riskier behaviors, which include gambling. Success in these domains is frequently equated with social prowess and masculinity, thus fostering a culture where gambling is celebrated among men. For women, however, gambling is less about proving prowess and more about coping. Here, social stigma plays a significant role. Women may experience judgment or shame for participating in gambling, especially when it crosses into addiction territory, forcing many to hide their habits and deal with these issues in isolation.

These differing engagements with gambling have important ramifications when we consider the rising accessibility of gambling through digital means. Online gambling platforms are reshaping the landscape, offering anonymity that might appeal more to women who wish to avoid societal scrutiny. This development not only influences how genders engage with gambling but also how addiction manifests and is identified – or overlooked – by loved ones and mental health practitioners.

In recognizing these nuances, it's crucial to understand that men and women may require different approaches in gambling addiction therapy and recovery. For men, strategies that focus on reducing competitive urges and increasing mindfulness can prove effective. Enhancing skills in self-regulation might reduce risky gambling behaviors driven by the need for control and excitement. Women, however, might benefit more from interventions that target emotional vulnerabilities and provide alternative avenues for social engagement and stress relief.

Therapists and intervention programs might also consider the role of gender-specific support groups. These provide safe spaces where individuals can express vulnerabilities, share experiences, and offer mutual support without facing gender-based stereotypes or stigmatization. Tailoring these groups to discuss personal experiences framed by gender can empower individuals by validating their unique experiences and responses to gambling.

The distinctions between how men and women gamble are more than just differences in preference or style; they are indicative of deeper, culturally ingrained values and psychological differences. Understanding these is pivotal not only for individuals grappling with gambling addiction but for society at large. This knowledge can drive more effective public health strategies and awareness campaigns that resonate with diverse audiences.

Indeed, as technology and societal norms continue to evolve, the patterns of gambling will undoubtedly shift. Yet, by recognizing and adapting to the unique needs and challenges faced by different genders, there is hope for more inclusive and effective means of combating gambling addiction. Embracing these differences paves the way for a more nuanced understanding of gambling and, ultimately, healthier approaches to both addiction prevention and recovery.

Societal Expectations

Societal expectations play a significant role in shaping gender differences in gambling behavior. Men and women are often subject to varied social norms and pressures, influencing not only how they gamble but also their motivations and the societal repercussions of their behaviors.

From an early age, traditional gender roles dictate what is considered acceptable behavior for males and females. For men, taking risks is often encouraged and seen as a mark of bravery and masculinity. This expectation can lead to a higher propensity for gambling, as men may view it as an avenue to demonstrate their risk-taking abilities. The thrill of gambling is frequently aligned with the societal image of men as daring and adventurous, reinforcing the behavior as congruent with what is socially expected.

In contrast, women often face a different set of societal pressures. Historically, femininity has been associated with stability, nurturing, and conservatism. Consequently, women who gamble might encounter a societal paradox. On one hand, they are encouraged to fit within traditional roles that emphasize carefulness and responsibility. On the other, they live in modern environments where independence and self-expression are becoming increasingly valued. This duality can lead to internal conflicts, where societal norms discourage gambling, yet individual autonomy invites it.

Moreover, societal expectations around gender not only affect why and how individuals gamble but also how their behaviors are perceived by others. Men who participate in gambling may face less social stigma than women. If a man loses money in gambling, it might be attributed to unlucky circumstances. In contrast, if a woman faces similar losses, she often might be viewed more harshly or judged for irresponsibility, reflecting enduring gender biases.

The media plays a crucial role in perpetuating these societal expectations. Gambling advertisements often depict male participants as bold strategists, while female participants may be portrayed with an emphasis on their novelty to the experience or as sideline observers. Such portrayals reinforce existing stereotypes and can influence societal perceptions. These narratives, when consumed repeatedly, can make it more challenging for individuals to see beyond traditional gender norms and determine their paths free from societal constraints.

Additionally, the spaces in which gambling occurs can reflect and reinforce societal expectations. Casinos and betting venues, traditionally viewed as male-dominated arenas, might not offer the same welcoming atmosphere for women. The perception of casinos as masculine spaces can exacerbate the reluctance of women to gamble, not solely due to the social risks associated with gambling itself but due to the perceived incongruence with female societal roles.

The impact of societal expectations on gambling is not merely theoretical. Research indicates that men are indeed more likely to develop gambling disorders compared to women, possibly reflecting these underlying societal prompts. However, it's essential to acknowledge that women are not immune to the appeal of gambling. The growth of online gambling platforms provides an environment where women might feel more protected from judgmental eyes, enabling participation away from socially constructed spaces.

Conversely, the private nature of online gambling can lead to other issues. The isolation inherent in these activities might exacerbate underlying mental health issues or increase susceptibility to addiction. This form of gambling can become an emotional escape, free from immediate societal judgment, but it often lacks the social oversight that might have acted as a deterrent in a communal setting.

Efforts towards gambling prevention and intervention must be mindful of these societal influences. Understanding the social contexts in which gambling behaviors are entrenched allows practitioners to tailor interventions that resonate with individuals on a personal level. This approach requires a shift—from solely focusing on the individual to considering the wider social narratives that shape behavior.

Creating supportive environments that challenge traditional gender norms can empower individuals to seek help without fear of stigma. Promoting narratives that encourage balanced risk-taking devoid of gendered labels can also help. Understanding societal expectations offers insight into deeper systemic issues, paving the way for more effective prevention and recovery strategies that are inclusive and empathetic.

As societal views continue to evolve, it's imperative to remain vigilant about how these changes impact gambling behaviors across genders. Researchers and practitioners need to remain attuned to these shifts, ensuring that approaches to gambling addiction continue to reflect a comprehensive understanding of the social fabric in which individuals exist. Empowering individuals by changing societal narratives around gender and gambling could not only mitigate the onset of gambling issues but also aid in building supportive networks conducive to recovery.

Chapter 13:
Age and Gambling

In exploring the relationship between age and gambling, we uncover a tapestry of influences that uniquely affect various age groups. Youth often find themselves lured by the thrill of gambling, misguided by a complex cocktail of bravado and naivete. With brains still in development, they show heightened vulnerability to the psychological hooks that gambling sets. Conversely, seniors, navigating through different life challenges, might turn to gambling as a means of socialization or distraction, sometimes with retirement funds at play. Both groups, susceptible in distinct ways, highlight the intricate ways that age and life stage interact with gambling tendencies. Understanding these connections is crucial not only for diagnosing potential gambling issues early but also for developing age-appropriate prevention and intervention strategies that savor potential futures untethered by the chains of addiction.

Youth Vulnerability

Gambling, at first glance, might seem like an adult pastime, laden with neon lights and loud casino floors, an exhilarating dive into risk and chance. However, it's in the finer crevices of society that a specter looms—a particular susceptibility that shadows our youth. Today's young people live in a world where the digital and the physical realms blur. Within this blend lies a newfound exposure to gambling, not just through brightly lit slot machines, but through intricate layers of online platforms, social media, and peer influences.

Their adolescent brains, still in the critical phases of development, are primed for exploration and novelty. This phase of life is characterized by seeking thrills and an innate desire to test boundaries. Neurobiologically, the prefrontal cortex—the region responsible for decision-making and impulse control—is still maturing, making youth particularly vulnerable to developing behaviors that straddle risk and reward. For many young individuals, the gap between understanding a calculated risk and succumbing to an addictive pattern can be perilously thin.

Moreover, technology plays a pivotal role in molding this vulnerability. In the digital age, gambling has seamlessly woven itself into the very fabric of online environments that young people frequent. Video games, social media, and apps introduce gambling elements like loot boxes and online betting, wrapping gambling in the guise of innocent play. The constant barrage of persuasive, often manipulative, digital content feeds their impressionable minds and can precipitate a slide into gambling behaviors. It's not uncommon for these environments to offer rewards that mimic real-world betting, yet without the immediate financial risks, allowing dangerous habits to foster.

The family environment also contributes to youth susceptibility to gambling. Children who grow up in households where gambling is a regular, perhaps even normalized, activity are at a higher risk. They observe these behaviors and internalize them, perceiving gambling as a mundane aspect of adult life. Simultaneously, parental gambling habits might alter family dynamics, potentially leading to disruptions that leave emotional voids in children, analogous to those discussed in the broader context of addiction. These voids often become a breeding ground for escapism through gambling.

Peer pressure and the desire for social acceptance can't be ignored either. As is crucial with many developmental challenges faced by youth, the social dimension significantly influences gambling behavior. Young people often crave belonging and might see gambling as a pathway to securing a spot in peer groups. This aspect is particularly concerning when gambling is positioned as a fashionable endeavor within social circles. The stakes, both literal and metaphorical, become an avenue to demonstrate bravery, success, or maturity falsely.

The consequences of early exposure to gambling behaviors stretch beyond mere financial implications; they can shape identity and future behaviors, instilling patterns that linger well into adulthood. These formative years are critical, and patterns established here can see the youth teetering on the edge of lifelong gambling addiction. Despite the allure of immediate rewards, the concept of fiscal responsibility and delayed gratification is often underdeveloped in adolescents, making long-term consequences difficult for them to comprehend fully.

Schools and educational institutions have the potential to play a changing role in combating youth gambling by facilitating awareness programs. Education, ideally tailored to resonate with adolescents, could illuminate the risks associated with gambling. Schools serve as more than venues of academic learning; they are crucial fields for social development, where prevention strategies can root resilience against gambling temptations.

There's an urgent need for dialogue and understanding among parents, educators, policymakers, and technology innovators. The dynamics of youth vulnerability to gambling are complex, often interwoven with ever-evolving technologies. Designing games and platforms in a way that acknowledges and mitigates these risks is a responsibility that needs to be embraced by those who manufacture and regulate them. Legislative oversight can also ensure that virtual gambling products do not slip through regulatory loopholes that shield traditional gambling practices from scrutiny.

Encouraging collaboration across sectors could lead to innovative solutions. Incorporating advanced analytics and data-driven insights into gaming platforms might provide proactive measures to identify and protect vulnerable users. Developers have the capacity, and arguably the ethical obligation, to embed safeguards that consider the psychological impact on younger audiences. Restrictive measures, educational pop-ups, and clear indications of spending could act as systemic deterrents.

Importantly, awareness must extend into the household as well. Families can be equipped with resources to detect early signs of gambling tendencies and to initiate conversations about this challenging topic. Fostering open communication lines within families about the realities and dangers of gambling can dismantle stigmas and provide much-needed support before gambling habits cement themselves into damaging addictions.

Lastly, professionals within psychology, addiction treatment, and behavioral sciences hold the responsibility to continuously explore and refine treatment and prevention strategies tailored for the youth. The naiveté and impulsivity inherent in youth demand a nuanced approach that recognizes the balance of guidance and autonomy. Creating spaces where young individuals can engage with support networks, learn coping mechanisms, and build resistance to potentially harmful behaviors is paramount.

The story of youth vulnerability to gambling mirrors a larger narrative that spans cultures and histories. It emphasizes a collective accountability to safeguard futures by addressing the contributing factors while championing innovative solutions. By shining a light on these vulnerabilities, there's an opportunity to not only prevent gambling addiction but to preserve the promise and potential that comes with youth.

Senior Gambling Patterns

As we delve deeper into the interplay between age and gambling, it becomes evident that senior gambling patterns deserve particular attention. For many older adults, gambling starts as a seemingly innocent pastime, a way to socialize and stave off the loneliness that can accompany aging. They often find themselves in casinos and bingo halls, where familiar faces and the prospect of a win add excitement to their routine. However, the activity can slowly morph from a leisure pursuit into something more problematic, with psychological, social, and financial implications.

The appeal of gambling for seniors is multifaceted. On one hand, it offers a social outlet—a break from isolation—especially for those who may have lost spouses or whose children live far away. Senior centers and community groups frequently arrange trips to casinos, which are seen as safe and welcoming environments. These outings often become cherished opportunities for connection. Yet, embedded within this desire for social interaction is the risk of developing unhealthy gambling behaviors, driven not only by loneliness but by other emotional voids and challenges, such as boredom or the need for excitement.

Moreover, gambling establishments are adept at catering to the senior demographic. Offers of free or discounted transportation, meals, and loyalty programs with points can be enticing. These marketing techniques are designed to create a comfortable environment where seniors feel valued and appreciated. Such attention can sometimes make it difficult to recognize when gambling has crossed the line from recreational to compulsive. As we examine the prevalence of senior gambling, it's important to consider how these external influences contribute to its allure.

Psychological factors play a significant role in shaping senior gambling patterns. As individuals age, they may encounter a series of life transitions—retirement, health issues, or bereavement—that influence their emotional landscape. Gambling can serve as a coping mechanism, a way to fill time, or avoid facing difficult emotions or realities. For some, the thrill of a win or the promise of a payout acts as a temporary balm, masking deeper issues that remain unaddressed. This reliance on gambling as a form of emotional escape is a crucial aspect of the addiction puzzle.

Additionally, cognitive changes that occur with aging may impact gambling behaviors. Decision-making capabilities can be affected, altering how seniors perceive risks and rewards. For instance, some may underestimate the odds due to a decrease in cognitive sharpness, or they may adhere to faulty belief systems about winning. This can lead them into patterns of chasing losses or escalating their bets in an attempt to recoup past losses—behaviors that significantly heighten the risk of developing a gambling disorder.

Financial security in older age is another aspect closely tied to senior gambling patterns. Many in this age group live on fixed incomes and face financial insecurity, making the prospect of a big win incredibly appealing. Unfortunately, this desire to alleviate financial concerns through gambling often results in the opposite, as losses accumulate and exacerbate the economic strain. The pressure to maintain a facade of financial stability can make it difficult for seniors to seek help, perpetuating a cycle of secrecy and addiction.

The intersection of gambling and mental health in seniors is particularly concerning. Depression and anxiety are common among older adults, and these conditions can both influence and be exacerbated by gambling behaviors. Seniors struggling with mental health issues may turn to gambling as a form of self-medication, further complicating the path to recovery. Addressing underlying mental health problems is essential in treating gambling disorders, highlighting the importance of integrated approaches that consider the whole person.

It's crucial to recognize that while problem gambling is a serious concern among seniors, the path to recovery and prevention is not without hope. Increased awareness, targeted interventions, and the development of senior-specific support systems can mitigate the risk factors at play. Empowering seniors through education about the realities of gambling odds, the risks associated with gambling, and the importance of seeking help early, can go a long way in reducing the prevalence of addiction.

Building resilience in seniors is also essential. Encouraging engagement in fulfilling, non-gambling activities can provide the social and emotional benefits they seek without the associated risks. Educational programs that focus on financial literacy and mental wellness can equip seniors with the tools they need to manage their time and emotions more effectively. Family members and caregivers also play a vital role in recognizing signs of gambling problems early and offering support in nonjudgmental ways.

In conclusion, understanding the unique factors that influence senior gambling patterns enables us to address this issue with empathy and knowledge. It's a multifaceted challenge that calls for a holistic approach, incorporating both prevention and recovery strategies tailored to the needs and experiences of older adults. By fostering a supportive environment and promoting awareness, we can help seniors maintain their well-being and avoid the pitfalls of gambling addiction, ensuring that their golden years are truly fulfilling and joyful.

Chapter 14:
The Path to Recovery

The journey to overcoming gambling addiction is as intricate as the human psyche itself, meandering through a landscape of challenges and triumphs, setbacks and revelations. It begins with the harder choice of facing the mirror, recognizing the powerful grip of addiction, and reaching out for a lifeline amidst the sinking sands of chaos. Recovery is rarely a linear path; rather, it's marked by stages of change where motivation waxes and wanes like the moon, casting shadows of doubt that must be met with persistent determination. Each step forward might veer into a relapse, testing one's resolve and demanding a deeper commitment to transformation. Yet, it's the unwavering belief in one's capacity to change and the courage to confront underlying emotional wounds that lay the foundation for lasting recovery. As one learns to navigate these pathways, embracing small victories and seeking support in community and therapy, they nurture resilience that ultimately leads to reclaiming control over their life. The path to recovery is a testament to the human spirit's remarkable ability to heal and thrive against the odds.

Stages of Change

In the journey towards recovery from gambling addiction, understanding the stages of change is paramount. This process doesn't happen overnight, and it's certainly not linear. Rather, recovery unfolds in a series of stages, each presenting its own challenges and triumphs. Recognizing which stage one is in can offer essential insights and guide actions toward positive transformations.

The first stage is **Precontemplation**, where individuals may not yet see their gambling as a problem. They might believe they have control or rationalize their behavior by pointing out wins or downplaying losses. This denial often creates a barrier to seeking help, as the individual does not yet perceive a need for change. For family and friends, this stage can be particularly frustrating, as they may see the warning signs that the gambler themselves cannot—or will not—acknowledge.

Moving forward, we encounter the stage of **Contemplation**. Here, individuals begin to recognize that their gambling may be problematic. It's a period characterized by a growing awareness of the negative consequences, such as financial strain or damaged relationships, yet it is still often marked by ambivalence. The person is considering the pros and cons of their behavior and contemplating change, though action has yet to be taken. At this juncture, motivational interviewing and empathetic support can be crucial in helping the individual weigh their options.

Subsequently, the **Preparation** stage is where plans start taking shape. In this phase, an individual is ready to make a change. They've assessed their situation, possibly even starting to seek support or gather information on treatment options. It's a hopeful period where the person builds the mental framework required to embark on the path to recovery. Small, incremental steps towards change, facilitated by professional guidance, can make the transition to the next stage easier.

The **Action** stage represents the moment when an individual begins to modify their behavior in earnest. They've often engaged in a treatment program, joined support groups, or set personal boundaries to limit gambling opportunities. This stage is characterized by a proactive approach, where real effort is dedicated to new patterns of behavior. Encouragement and tangible support are critical during this time as the person navigates the often challenging shift between old habits and new, healthier ones.

Following this is the stage of **Maintenance**, where sustaining the new behavior becomes the primary focus. Individuals work to solidify their gains and develop strategies to prevent relapse. This period is crucial because the risk of reverting to old habits can be high, especially when facing triggers or stressors. Continuous support, whether from professionals or peer networks, can bolster resilience and help maintain the hard-won changes.

Finally, while not always included in every model, **Relapse** is often considered an integral stage of change in addiction recovery. It's a recognition that falling back into old behaviors is common, not a failure, and certainly not the end of the road. Relapses provide valuable lessons, highlighting areas that need further work or new strategies. Individuals can, and often do, regain their footing with renewed commitment to the path of recovery.

Understanding and navigating these stages demands patience and persistence. Each stage presents unique psychological challenges and offers opportunities for growth. By recognizing where one stands in this process, individuals can more effectively address gambling addiction and move towards a healthier, more fulfilling life. Through empathy and support, both self-given and from others, the journey through the stages of change can be transformative, leading not only to recovery but to renewed self-awareness and stronger resolve in overcoming life's hurdles.

As we reflect on the stages of change, it becomes evident that change is deeply personal and varies widely from person to person. The path to recovery is as unique as the individuals undertaking it, marked by personal insights, struggles, and achievements. Despite the challenges that lie in each stage, the potential for change remains a powerful and attainable goal—one that promises a life where gambling no longer holds sway over one's choices and future.

Overcoming Relapse

Relapse can be a daunting word for anyone on the path to recovery from gambling addiction. However, it's crucial to understand that relapses, while concerning, are not signs of failure but rather part of the recovery journey. The challenge is in learning from them, understanding their triggers, and developing strategies to prevent them in the future.

In many cases, relapse stems from unaddressed emotional triggers or unresolved psychological issues. The feelings of anxiety, depression, or even boredom can often drive individuals back to the familiar escape that gambling provides. It's essential for individuals to work closely with therapists and support groups to identify the underlying emotions that can lead them back to destructive behaviors. Recognizing these emotions can empower individuals to face them head-on, rather than masking them with gambling.

Relapse doesn't happen overnight. It usually begins with subtle shifts in behavior or mindset—small rationalizations that gambling might 'just this once' help alleviate stress or provide a much-needed thrill. Being cognizant of these thoughts is the first step in prevention. One effective approach is to keep a journal of gambling urges and the situations that prompt them. By documenting these instances, individuals can start to see patterns and preemptively tackle the situations that could lead to relapse.

Peer support is another critically important component in overcoming relapse. Sharing experiences with others who have faced similar struggles provides a sense of belonging and understanding. Support groups offer a space free of judgment where members can express their fears and setbacks and also hear how others navigated their journeys back to recovery. These interactions often plant the seeds of resilience, highlighting that every slip can be met with a comeback.

Moreover, constructing a robust support system outside of organized groups is key. Family and friends can play a vital role in providing encouragement and accountability. Open communication with trusted loved ones about one's struggles and victories fosters an environment where relapse is less likely to thrive. Establishing clear and sometimes tough boundaries with those in one's social circle is also vital for staying on course. They need to understand the significance of offering unwavering support without enabling old habits.

Mindfulness and stress reduction techniques can't be overlooked. Practices like meditation, yoga, or deep breathing exercises provide individuals with tools to manage cravings and reduce stress. By focusing on the present moment and acknowledging urges without acting on them, individuals can gradually diminish the power these urges hold. Additionally, physical activity, art, or music can serve as healthy outlets to channel energies that might otherwise lead to gambling.

Additionally, practical strategies, such as financial management and planning, are essential in the fight against relapse. Developing a structured, real-life approach by setting limits, removing access to credit, and involving a trusted person to oversee finances enhances awareness and accountability. This not only aids in preventing impulsive decisions but also reintroduces stability into one's life, which is often disrupted by gambling activities.

It's crucial to focus on redefining one's relationship with leisure and fun. Finding new hobbies, engaging in sports, or adopting creative projects can fill the void gambling once held. By replacing it with constructive and fulfilling activities, the reliance on gambling for entertainment diminishes. This shift helps foster a sense of satisfaction and accomplishment that is sustainable and healthy.

Above all, patience and self-compassion are vital. The road to recovery isn't linear, and setbacks are part of the learning process. Each step away from gambling, however small, is a step towards a healthier, more fulfilling life. Rather than internalizing guilt over a relapse, viewing it as an opportunity to learn and grow reinforces strength and perseverance on the path to recovery.

By confronting relapse with strategic measures, holistic approaches, and a supportive network, individuals can not just overcome setbacks but emerge stronger. The courage to face these challenges head-on and the commitment to continuous personal growth can transform the seemingly insurmountable hurdles of relapse into stepping stones towards sustained recovery and fulfillment.

Chapter 15:
Therapeutic Approaches

Addressing gambling addiction effectively requires a nuanced understanding of therapeutic approaches tailored to the individual's unique needs. Cognitive Behavioral Therapy (CBT) stands at the forefront, helping individuals challenge and alter distorted thinking patterns that fuel their addictive behaviors. By focusing on the 'here and now', CBT encourages clients to reframe harmful thoughts and develop healthier coping mechanisms. Group support and counseling offer an additional layer of healing, providing communal reinforcement where individuals can share experiences, gain insights, and draw strength from shared struggles. Such environments facilitate connection, reduce isolation, and foster accountability—key components in a recovery journey. Therapeutic interventions, adaptable and personalized, serve as vital tools in the multifaceted battle against gambling addiction, illuminating paths toward restoration and resilience.

Cognitive Behavioral Therapy

The journey towards recovery from gambling addiction is as complex as the addiction itself. Cognitive Behavioral Therapy (CBT) has emerged as a leading therapeutic approach, hailed for its practical and structured methodology in addressing the psychological underpinnings of gambling addiction. But what makes CBT particularly effective? At its core, CBT focuses on the intricate relationship between thoughts, emotions, and behaviors. For individuals struggling with gambling addiction, this means exploring how distorted thinking patterns can fuel compulsive gambling behavior.

CBT operates on the premise that our thoughts drive our feelings, which in turn influence our actions. In the context of gambling, this might manifest as distorted beliefs about one's ability to control the outcome of games or minimizing the negative consequences of gambling. By identifying and challenging these cognitive distortions, CBT helps individuals develop more rational and balanced thoughts. This process involves a collaborative effort between the therapist and the patient. Together, they embark on a journey to dissect and reconstruct the addictive behaviors into healthier patterns.

A distinctive feature of CBT is its time-limited and goal-oriented nature. Typically, treatment sessions span over a few weeks to months, providing a focused framework for recovering individuals. The therapy is structured with specific measurable goals, which are tailored to address the unique challenges faced by each individual. This structure provides patients with a sense of progress and achievement, which bolsters their motivation and commitment to change.

Moreover, CBT isn't just about addressing the negative thoughts and behaviors associated with gambling. It's also about equipping individuals with coping strategies to manage stress, anxiety, and other triggers that may lead to gambling. Techniques such as relaxation exercises, problem-solving skills, and developing new hobbies are integrated into the therapy, providing a holistic approach to recovery. By learning these strategies, individuals gain resilience, which is crucial in resisting the urges to gamble.

CBT also emphasizes the importance of self-monitoring and reflection. Patients are encouraged to keep a diary of their gambling activities, thoughts, and emotions. This ongoing self-reflection is pivotal; it allows them to recognize patterns and triggers that they might not be aware of initially. This heightened awareness can serve as a deterrent, as individuals see firsthand the links between their thoughts and gambling behaviors.

Another strength of CBT lies in its adaptability. It can be customized to meet the diverse needs of individuals, whether they're young or old, experienced gamblers or novices. This flexibility is why CBT is widely adopted in therapeutic settings around the world. It's effective not only in one-on-one sessions but also in group therapy settings. In group settings, individuals can share their experiences and strategies, offering mutual support that can foster a sense of community and shared mission towards recovery.

Importantly, CBT recognizes and addresses the emotional void that gambling often seeks to fill. Through exploring and unpacking emotions, individuals can identify what truly drives their gambling behavior. They may discover it's not just about the thrill or the potential financial gain but about escaping from unresolved feelings of loneliness, depression, or anxiety. CBT provides a safe space for these emotions to be acknowledged and processed, without the need to escape through gambling.

For many individuals, gambling is more than just a habit; it becomes a way of coping with life's challenges. CBT helps to shift this perspective, guiding individuals to see gambling for what it truly is: a temporary fix that ultimately compounds problems. This realization is pivotal in breaking the cycle of addiction and forging a path towards sustainable healing.

In conclusion, Cognitive Behavioral Therapy offers a robust framework for understanding and overcoming the intricate psychological mechanisms that underpin gambling addiction. It empowers individuals to confront their thoughts and behaviors, replacing destructive patterns with healthier alternatives. For anyone caught in the grips of gambling addiction, CBT presents not just a method of treatment, but a beacon of hope and a practical pathway to long-term recovery. It's about reclaiming one's life, one thoughtful decision at a time.

Group Support and Counseling

Group support and counseling play a vital role in the therapeutic landscape for gambling addiction. Human connection and collective experience provide a unique form of healing that's often missing in individual therapy. It creates a space where individuals don't just talk; they listen, learn, and grow together. In a group setting, participants feel less isolated as they hear others voice similar struggles and victories. This shared journey can fortify personal resolve and illuminate avenues for recovery previously hidden.

Engaging with a group offers multiple perspectives, broadening one's understanding of the issues at hand. When someone shares their story, it often resonates with others, reflecting their internal struggles and triumphs. This collective narrative helps individuals realize they're not alone in their experiences, fostering a sense of community and belonging. For many, this communal validation can be a critical balm against the stigma and shame associated with gambling addiction.

The structure of group counseling can vary significantly, but most follow a framework that combines openness with confidentiality. Some groups may be facilitated by a professional therapist who guides discussions, introduces themes, and suggests coping strategies. Others rely on peer leadership, with members volunteering to lead sessions and share personal insights. Both formats have merits, offering different dynamics that cater to various needs and preferences within the group.

One significant advantage of group support is peer accountability. When individuals commit to regular attendance and participation, they're more likely to stay aligned with their recovery goals. The act of checking in with others, sharing progress, and facing gentle, supportive questioning can enhance personal accountability. This dynamic reinforces personal commitment and helps mitigate the risk of relapse.

Counseling within a group context often integrates various therapeutic techniques. Motivational interviewing might be used to help members identify personal goals and understand their ambivalence about change. Cognitive Behavioral Therapy (CBT) components could be introduced to challenge and reshape destructive thought patterns. In blending these approaches, group counseling becomes a versatile and adaptive tool, offering insight and strategies tailored to the collective experience but beneficial individually.

Stories of personal transformation within groups are prevalent and persuasive. Participants often recount that the turning point in their recovery came from a group interaction that either profoundly moved them or challenged them to think differently. It's within this space that lightbulb moments occur — when a comment or an anecdote catalyzes deep reflection or sparks a newfound determination. The weight of shared experiences often underscores these epiphanies, making them more impactful.

It's crucial also to acknowledge the emotional safety a well-structured group provides. Members voice vulnerabilities, seek guidance, and offer support, knowing they are met with empathy rather than judgment. This environment cultivates trust, a foundational element for meaningful change and recovery. The therapist or facilitator's role is to maintain this safe space, ensuring that each member feels valued and heard.

While group counseling is a potent modality, it's not without challenges. Sessions may trigger intense emotions, bringing unresolved issues to the forefront. Members might struggle with feelings of vulnerability or discomfort as they confront their behaviors and understandings. However, these challenges are often stepping stones toward personal growth. An effective group guides participants through these choppy waters with sensitivity and skill, transforming potential setbacks into opportunities for insight.

Moreover, the diversity within a group can enhance the recovery experience by exposing individuals to a tapestry of life experiences and coping mechanisms. Members learn not just from their own journey but from the collective wisdom and diverse stories shared in the room. This dynamic exchange enriches the therapeutic process, offering multiple pathways to understanding and healing.

The integration of online platforms for group support and counseling has expanded access to these valuable resources. Virtual groups break down geographical barriers, allowing individuals to connect who might otherwise have limited opportunities to participate in such recovery communities. While the online format poses unique challenges, such as fostering connection and maintaining engagement, it equally offers anonymity and convenience that can encourage participation.

In conclusion, group support and counseling provide a multifaceted approach to treating gambling addiction. They contribute uniquely to the recovery process by weaving together individual narratives into a collective fabric of understanding and resilience. The synergy generated in these groups propels personal growth, provides valued support, and nurtures accountability, all essential elements for long-term recovery success. As we consider the path to healing from gambling addiction, it's clear that the power of community is both fundamental and transformative.

Chapter 16:
The Role of Family in Recovery

Family serves as a vital cornerstone in the journey to overcoming gambling addiction, providing both a support system and a catalyst for change. When a family member is caught in the throes of this addiction, the impact ripples through the entire household, disrupting relationships and eroding trust. Yet, this shared struggle can foster immense opportunities for growth and healing. Family interventions often play a key role in encouraging the individual to seek help and stick with recovery programs. By understanding the complexities of gambling addiction and being equipped with empathy and effective communication strategies, families can transform into a powerful source of motivation and accountability. The collective journey towards recovery becomes less daunting when family members educate themselves about the addiction's psychological triggers and cooperate in constructing a supportive environment. Through patience and mutual understanding, families can not only mend the fractures caused by addiction but also build a more resilient foundation for the future.

Family Interventions

Family plays a pivotal role in the recovery from gambling addiction, and family interventions can serve as a crucial turning point for individuals caught in the cycle of addiction. The intricacies of family dynamics often contribute to the complexity of gambling addiction, making the involvement of family members an essential component of a comprehensive recovery plan. When family members understand the nature of addiction and actively participate in interventions, they can provide the necessary emotional support and accountability that foster healing.

An effective family intervention starts with education. Families need to understand that gambling addiction is a mental health disorder, not a mere lack of self-control or a moral failing. By dispelling myths and misconceptions, families can shift from judgment to empathy. This perspective change is paramount, as it creates a non-judgmental environment conducive to open communication. Family members who are educated on the psychological triggers, such as emotional voids or reinforcement schedules, can better understand their loved one's struggles.

Once the family has a basic understanding, structuring a formal intervention is often the next step. These interventions need careful planning with the guidance of a professional, like a counselor or a therapist. The presence of a neutral third-party can defuse tensions and guide the process to ensure it remains constructive. During the intervention, family members express their concerns directly but compassionately, emphasizing their unconditional support for the recovery journey.

It's essential to involve all family members in the intervention, as each person can play a different but significant role. Some may offer emotional support, while others might provide practical help like managing finances. The collective effort of the family underscores the message that the individual is not alone in their struggle. This support network can be remarkably motivating, offering the addicted person a sense of belonging and reassurance needed to pursue treatment seriously.

Alongside interventions, continuous family therapy can facilitate ongoing recovery. Such therapy sessions can improve communication, resolve conflicts, and build healthier patterns of interaction that prevent relapse. As family members learn more about both addiction and their own responses to it, they can contribute to a nurturing environment that helps the addicted individual remain in recovery. Strong family support often translates into stronger commitment from the individual to stick with treatment programs.

While interventions are beneficial, they can also uncover complex emotions and historical tensions within families. Past grievances, feelings of betrayal, and mistrust might surface, making some interactions challenging. Therapists often find that addressing these underlying issues can be as critical as tackling the addiction itself. By resolving these conflicts, the family can emerge stronger and more united, offering a robust support system that benefits everyone involved.

Financial difficulties often accompany gambling addiction. Family interventions may include devising a strategic plan to manage finances better. This might involve assigning financial responsibilities to someone trustworthy until the individual regains control. Such practical steps lessen the severity of gambling's impact, preventing further damage while enabling the individual to focus on recovery.

Additionally, involving family members in prevention strategies can highlight the importance of setting boundaries and rules that discourage gambling behaviors. Families that communicate openly about financial goals and emotional well-being are often better at recognizing potential triggers. They can act swiftly to address them, contributing to the prevention of relapse.

However, not all family members may be equipped to participate effectively in interventions due to their own emotions or misunderstandings about addiction. In such cases, educating them through workshops, support groups, or literature can enhance their ability to contribute positively. Recognizing that each family member's journey in understanding and dealing with gambling addiction is unique can help reduce frustration and promote a more supportive atmosphere.

Family interventions are not just about correcting behavior but also about healing relationships. When family members commit to collective healing, they tackle not only the gambling problem but also the familial issues that might have contributed to it. This holistic approach allows families to build resilience against future challenges, whether related to gambling or other adversities.

It's important to note that the effectiveness of family interventions varies. For some, these interventions might catalyze recovery, while for others, they could initiate a long, ongoing process of healing. The key is persistence and the willingness to adapt strategies as needed. A family's unwavering support can strengthen an individual's determination to overcome addiction and can significantly impact their path to recovery.

The role of family in recovery can't be overstated. Through strategic and compassionate interventions, families don't just help break the cycle of gambling addiction; they also foster an environment of love, understanding, and support that aids in the long-term well-being of their loved ones. The journey of recovery is undoubtedly personal, but with family by their side, individuals battling gambling addiction have a sturdy foundation upon which they can build a healthier future.

Supporting a Loved One

When a family member struggles with gambling addiction, it can feel like you're navigating an emotional minefield. The desire to help is often intertwined with feelings of frustration, anger, and helplessness. Yet, supporting a loved one through recovery is invaluable and can significantly enhance their chances of breaking free from the clutches of addiction. This support, however, needs to be thoughtful, informed, and compassionate.

The first step in supporting a loved one is acquiring knowledge about gambling addiction. Understanding that it's not merely a lack of willpower but a complex psychological condition helps in being more empathetic. Educating oneself about the triggers, the signs of relapse, and the emotional challenges involved lays a foundation for effective support. It also empowers family members to step into discussions with a better grasp, reducing the risk of alienating the individual grappling with addiction.

Communication plays a pivotal role in this support system. Establishing an open, non-judgmental line of communication can foster trust and encourage your loved one to share their struggles without the fear of being condemned. Often, individuals suffering from addiction may feel ashamed or isolated due to stigma. By being present and offering a listening ear, you provide a safe space for them to express themselves. It's important to focus on expressing concern and love rather than anger or disappointment.

Moreover, setting boundaries is crucial. While it may seem counterintuitive, creating clear, compassionate boundaries helps in maintaining a healthy dynamic and prevents enabling behavior. This means not just turning a blind eye to harmful gambling behaviors or bailing them out financially without considering the long-term implications. It's about demonstrating that you care about their well-being and are committed to their recovery, but you will not support activities that are harmful.

Engaging in family therapy can be transformative. Therapy provides a platform where family members can express their feelings and learn healthier ways of interaction. It also opens the door for the addicted family member to hear how their actions affect those around them. Therapists can facilitate discussions that might be too difficult to initiate at home, helping families develop strategies that promote recovery and understanding.

It's equally important for family members to take care of their own mental health. Supporting someone through addiction recovery can be emotionally exhausting. Seeking support from peer groups or therapists ensures that your emotional reservoir is replenished. Groups like Gam-Anon are designed for family and friends of individuals with gambling problems and can provide a community of understanding and shared experiences.

Encouraging healthy habits is another way to support recovery. This can be done by including your loved one in physical activities, creative pursuits, or social gatherings that distract from gambling. Helping them discover new interests and build a life that is fulfilling outside of gambling can reduce the temptation to return to it. These activities not only divert attention from gambling but also help in rebuilding self-esteem and confidence.

Financial counseling can also be beneficial. Gambling addiction often leaves behind significant financial turmoil. Assisting your loved one in seeking professional financial advice can help them learn to manage their finances responsibly. This not only alleviates some of the stress associated with accumulated debt but also teaches them a vital skill for maintaining their newfound stability.

Patience is key throughout the recovery process. Change doesn't happen overnight, and there will likely be setbacks. It's essential to celebrate small victories and progress even if they seem minor in the grand scheme. Encouragement and ongoing support need to be sustained over the long term, recognizing that recovery is a journey with many phases.

As much as your loved one needs support, it's crucial to acknowledge their autonomy and hold them accountable for their recovery. They need to actively participate in their treatment plans and support networks. By gently pushing them towards independence, you help fortify the internal motivations that are necessary for long-lasting change.

In conclusion, supporting a loved one through gambling addiction recovery is challenging yet incredibly rewarding. It requires a delicate balance of understanding, patience, and firmness. By equipping yourself with knowledge, maintaining healthy communication, setting boundaries, and encouraging professional help, you become a cornerstone in their path to recovery. Remember, you're part of a wider network of support that includes professionals and support groups, all dedicated to paving a healthier future for your loved one. Together, the journey towards recovery becomes a shared endeavor, illuminated by hope, resilience, and the enduring support of family.

Chapter 17:
Prevention Strategies

Prevention strategies are pivotal in reducing the onset of gambling addiction, focusing on strengthening awareness and resilience within individuals and communities. By incorporating comprehensive education programs that dissect the psychological allure and risks associated with gambling, we equip individuals with the knowledge needed to spot early warning signs and make informed decisions. Moreover, fostering resilience through targeted interventions helps individuals build coping mechanisms and emotional intelligence, enabling them to withstand the seductive pull of gambling. The implementation of these strategies within educational institutions, workplaces, and community-based organizations can create environments that promote healthy attitudes towards risk-taking and self-control. Ultimately, thorough prevention strategies pave the path towards a more informed society, curbing the cycle of addiction before it takes root and offering hope for sustainable change.

Education and Awareness

Understanding gambling addiction begins with a comprehensive approach to education and awareness. It's not just about imparting knowledge, but also about fostering a deeper self-awareness that allows individuals to recognize the subtle signs and behaviors that indicate susceptibility to gambling's seductive pull. Education serves as the first line of defense; it equips people with the tools to question their relationship with gambling in a meaningful way. By challenging misconceptions and breaking down the complex web of psychological triggers, educational initiatives can demystify the allure that many find hard to resist.

The process of education involves dissecting the complexities of how gambling affects the human mind. It requires moving beyond simple informational campaigns to immersive experiences that highlight the personal and societal impacts of gambling. Courses, workshops, and seminars can play a crucial role in this regard. Through interactive discussions and real-life case studies, individuals can better grasp why they are drawn to gambling and what happens once that line into addiction is crossed. It transforms abstract statistics into tangible realities, making the consequences of gambling addiction both visible and visceral.

Digital platforms have emerged as powerful tools in dispersing educational content regarding gambling addiction. Websites, apps, and online modules can reach a broader audience, offering self-paced learning opportunities. These resources not only educate but also engage users with compelling narratives that reflect their own experiences, bridging the gap between academic knowledge and personal insight. Video content, particularly, can break down complex theories into digestible segments, making it accessible to people from all walks of life.

An essential component in prevention is raising awareness among young people. The younger generations are often more susceptible due to their greater exposure to gambling through technology and social media. Schools and colleges can incorporate modules that discuss gambling addiction as part of their health and social education programs. These platforms can introduce students to the risks associated with gambling and equip them to make informed decisions.

Education in these formative years can act as a preventive measure, reducing the likelihood of future addiction.

Another key aspect is understanding cultural perceptions around gambling. Awareness initiatives should be culturally sensitive, recognizing that attitudes towards gambling can vary significantly across different communities. By tailoring educational content to respect these differences, we foster inclusivity, ensuring that the message resonates more deeply. Culturally aware campaigns can also remove stigma, encouraging more open conversations without fear of judgment or misunderstanding.

Community engagement is critical for spreading awareness. Local community centers, religious organizations, and social clubs can serve as effective platforms for discussions and workshops. These settings provide safe spaces where people feel comfortable sharing their experiences and concerns. By involving community leaders and influencers, these narratives become anchored in the community's fabric, encouraging others to come forward and seek help if needed.

Parents and family members also play an instrumental role in education and awareness. They can be educated to recognize early signs of gambling addiction, which often manifest subtly, such as secretive behavior or unexplained financial issues. Providing resources to families helps in creating a supportive environment that encourages open communication. Education doesn't stop at recognizing the problem; it extends to learning how to support one another effectively through the recovery process, emphasizing resilience and healthy coping mechanisms.

Moreover, confronting the stigma associated with gambling addiction is paramount. Many individuals shy away from seeking help due to fear of being judged or misunderstood. Educational initiatives can normalize addiction as a medical issue rather than a moral failing, thus reducing the associated shame and encouraging more people to seek help. This shift in narrative is foundational to building an empathy-driven approach, where addiction is met with support rather than discrimination.

Workplace education programs also hold promise. Companies can implement training sessions that educate employees on recognizing the signs of gambling addiction among colleagues and in themselves. Such programs not only enhance personal understanding and empathy but also promote a healthier work environment. They communicate that the organization stands ready to support employees facing gambling-related challenges.

Finally, media campaigns can play a powerful part in raising public awareness. Thought-provoking advertisements and documentaries can stimulate public interest and discussion, thereby dispelling myths associated with gambling addiction. Highlighting stories of recovery and hope can inspire individuals who are struggling to take the first step towards seeking help, showing them that recovery is not only possible but within reach.

In conclusion, education and awareness are fundamental components in the broader strategy to prevent gambling addiction. By leveraging multiple platforms and approaches, we can address the intricacies of gambling addiction while promoting a culture of understanding and solidarity. This holistic approach not only equips individuals with necessary knowledge but also strengthens community bonds, creating an environment where prevention and support walk hand in hand.

Building Resilience

In the journey to understanding and preventing gambling addiction, building resilience is essential. Resilience, often described as the ability to bounce back from adversity, plays a crucial role in safeguarding individuals against the pitfalls of addiction. It acts as a buffer, providing the psychological strength needed to resist the lure of gambling's false promises and the inevitable setbacks that accompany recovery attempts.

The concept of resilience isn't just about withstanding stress but actively transforming negative experiences into growth opportunities. For individuals grappling with the temptations of gambling, it involves cultivating skills and attitudes that empower them to navigate challenges and maintain a balanced life. This ability to adapt is not innate but can be developed through intentional practices and mindset shifts.

One of the primary components of resilience is self-awareness. Understanding one's triggers and vulnerabilities can make a significant difference in combating gambling addiction. By acknowledging patterns in behavior and emotional responses, individuals are better equipped to implement strategies that curb the desire to gamble. Self-awareness fosters a deeper comprehension of personal boundaries and risk factors.

Self-regulation is another critical facet of building resilience. It's about managing emotional responses and exercising control over impulses, which are often hijacked during the throes of gambling urges. Practical methods, such as mindfulness and meditation, can enhance self-regulation. These practices encourage individuals to remain present and grounded, offering a reprieve from the chaotic allure of gambling.

Beyond the internal strategies, social support systems play a pivotal role in fostering resilience. A network of understanding and supportive relationships—be it family, friends, or peer groups—provides encouragement and accountability. These connections furnish a safety net, reminding those at risk that they are not isolated in their struggle.

Sharing experiences and challenges can lighten the emotional burden and inspire hope.

Moreover, a resilient mindset often embraces flexibility and adaptability. Life is unpredictable, and setbacks are common. It's essential to view these challenges as temporary obstacles rather than insurmountable barriers. By shifting perspectives, individuals can learn to adapt to life's changes without resorting to gambling as a coping mechanism.

Cognitive restructuring is another powerful tool in the resilience-building arsenal. It involves challenging and changing negative thought patterns that can lead to gambling. This method encourages a more realistic appraisal of situations, empowering individuals to overcome cognitive biases that exaggerate the supposed benefits of gambling. Since cognitive distortions are deeply ingrained in gambling addiction, addressing them can mitigate the compulsion to gamble.

Physical well-being is also intrinsically linked to resilience. Regular exercise, a balanced diet, and adequate sleep contribute to overall mental health and can provide the energy and clarity needed to resist gambling urges. These foundational elements support both emotional stability and physical vigor, equipping individuals with the endurance required for long-term recovery.

Incorporating goal setting into the resilience-building process can guide individuals away from gambling tendencies. Establishing realistic and meaningful goals can instill a sense of purpose, motivating those at risk to focus on positive achievements rather than the transient thrill of gambling. This goal-oriented approach provides structure and direction, countering the aimless pursuit of gambling gratification.

Finally, fostering resilience involves embracing a sense of gratitude and optimism. Cultivating an appreciation for life's positive aspects can shift focus away from the need for external validation or excitement that gambling seeks to fill. Emphasizing optimism about personal growth and future possibilities can inspire those struggling with addiction to remain committed to their recovery journey.

Building resilience isn't a singular event but an ongoing process. It's about continuous growth and the integration of new skills into daily life. Through self-awareness, social support, mental flexibility, and positive lifestyle choices, individuals can develop a resilient shield that protects against the urge to gamble. This resilience becomes both a preventative strategy and a cornerstone for sustaining recovery.

Chapter 18:
Policy and Regulation

As we delve into the intricate web of policies and regulations surrounding gambling, it's clear that these measures aim to balance the thrill of gaming with the pressing need for public welfare. While legislation often serves as a double-edged sword, attempting to curb addiction while permitting personal freedom, its role is undeniably pivotal in shaping how society navigates the risks involved. Rigorous laws and prudent advertising restrictions are central to crafting environments where potential harm is minimized, yet they must continually evolve in response to technological advances and shifting cultural mores. Having workable policies is not just about setting boundaries; it finds an empathetic understanding of the psychological underpinnings of addiction and strives to build a framework that both prevents vulnerability and empowers recovery. Only through nuanced policy-making—attuned to diverse human experiences—can we aspire to foster a safer, healthier landscape in the realm of gambling.

Gambling Legislation

Gambling legislation stands at the intersection of public welfare and personal freedom, wielding the power to shape the societal landscape. In essence, it can be a cornerstone in combating gambling addiction. Across the globe, regulatory frameworks have been established with varying levels of stringency, reflecting cultural nuances and differing attitudes towards chance and risk. By dissecting these laws, we can begin to understand how they might serve as either barriers or catalysts to gambling addiction.

At the heart of gambling legislation is the intent to strike a balance between protecting individuals from potential harm and allowing for personal freedom and economic benefits. This delicate equilibrium is often reflected in the rigorous processes countries undergo to enact gambling laws. Such legislation typically covers who can gamble, where gambling can occur, and the types of games or bets that are permissible. Some regions opt for a liberal approach, allowing widespread availability of gambling facilities, while others restrict it to tightly controlled environments, often state-run, to minimize harm.

Regulation also serves as a mechanism for generating public revenue. Governments often find themselves in a moral debate: encouraging a lucrative industry that can simultaneously spark social issues. They attempt to alleviate potential harms through taxation and strict oversight, directing the funds towards public health initiatives and addiction services. This dual nature of gambling legislation, serving both regulatory and economic functions, underscores its complexity.

However, it's not just about legality or restriction. Many laws aim to ensure fairness, transparency, and the protection of gamblers. For example, regulations might mandate clear information regarding the odds of games, which helps dismantle myths that the house edge is an insurmountable foe or that skill alone can ensure a win. This aligns legislative action with educational endeavors, attempting to arm individuals with knowledge to prevent addiction.

The age restriction is a universal feature in global gambling laws, barring minors from engaging in such risky behavior. However, enforcing these restrictions remains a challenge. The rise of online and mobile gambling platforms further complicates matters, as digital anonymity can enable underage individuals to bypass these safeguards. Hence, legislation often extends to digital realms, requiring stringent identity checks and proof of age to access online gambling sites.

Importantly, gambling legislation is not static. It evolves in response to changing societal attitudes, emerging technologies, and new insights into addiction science. For instance, certain jurisdictions have introduced measures specifically targeting the explosive growth of online gambling. These policies might include imposing limits on maximum bets or losses, mandating self-exclusion options, and requiring operators to provide resources for seeking help.

Moreover, advertising restrictions have become a fundamental part of gambling legislation. The aim is to curtail the glamorization of gambling, which can lead to an increase in addiction. Advertisements are often banned from being aired during hours when minors might be exposed, and they are required to carry messages about the risks associated with gambling. Some jurisdictions have taken further steps to ban celebrity endorsements and sponsorships in gambling advertisements.

The international landscape reveals striking contrasts in approaches to gambling laws. While some countries adopt a prohibitionist stance, believing it to be the best deterrent against addiction, others view regulated gambling as a more pragmatic approach. Notably, countries like Singapore and Japan have emerged with innovative frameworks known as "integrated resorts," which couple gambling facilities with tourism and recreational attractions under strict regulation. These models aim to contain gambling within larger ecosystems, thus diffusing potential harms.

Behaviors and perceptions shift as policymakers adapt to new challenges, such as the burgeoning presence of cryptocurrencies and blockchain gambling. These technologies introduce complexities in regulation, including ensuring fair play and tackling money laundering. Gambling legislation must therefore continuously adapt, providing novel solutions to emerging issues while safeguarding public interests.

International organizations and collaborations also play a role in shaping gambling legislation. The exchange of ideas and successful practices among countries contributes to more robust legal frameworks globally. Such collaborative efforts inform initiatives aimed at standardizing regulations to address cross-border gambling activities, which have become more prevalent with internet accessibility.

Ultimately, the efficacy of gambling legislation in curbing addiction is a hotbed of debate. Some argue that such laws can effectively limit availability and mitigate harm, while others question their impact, suggesting that addiction finds ways to thrive regardless. What's clear, though, is that legislation alone cannot eradicate gambling addiction. It can lay the groundwork, create barriers, and provide support mechanisms, but societal changes and individual choices play an equally crucial role.

Thus, as we continue to explore the intricate dynamics of gambling addiction, understanding and refining legislation must remain a priority. It's a pivotal factor in a comprehensive strategy to mitigate the addictive pull of gambling, protecting individuals and communities while navigating the fine line between liberty and social accountability.

Advertising Restrictions

In today's hyper-connected world, the pervasive reach of advertising touches every aspect of our lives. For gambling, this reach becomes particularly significant as it navigates a delicate balance between promotion and regulation. Understanding the nuances of advertising restrictions in the realm of gambling is crucial, especially for those affected by gambling addiction and the professionals working to mitigate its impact.

The primary goal of advertising restrictions in gambling is to protect vulnerable populations while allowing industry stakeholders to operate within a regulated framework. These restrictions aim to minimize the risk of encouraging compulsive gambling behaviors, particularly among those prone to addiction. Policymakers, psychologists, and addiction specialists agree that aggressive or misleading advertising can trigger psychological mechanisms that lead to harmful gambling habits.

Regulatory bodies have implemented an array of advertising restrictions to ensure that gambling promotions are responsible and fair. One common measure is the imposition of strict guidelines on the content of advertisements. These guidelines often prohibit the depiction of gambling as a solution to financial difficulties or a means to achieve social status. Furthermore, advertisements should not target minors or imply that gambling can boost self-esteem or enhance personal qualities.

Besides content-specific restrictions, many jurisdictions enforce rules on the timing and placement of gambling advertisements. Limitations are often placed on when such ads can be broadcast on television or radio, commonly restricting them to late-night hours when fewer young audiences are watching. Additionally, preventing advertisements in locations known to attract a younger crowd, such as near schools or playgrounds, is a common strategic approach. Online platforms, too, are subject to these standards, with increasing emphasis on controlling digital marketing techniques that are easily accessible to minors.

The rise of digital and interactive media continues to challenge regulators, who must adapt quickly to technological advancements.

Online gambling ads, driven by data analytics and personalized targeting, can easily circumvent traditional restrictions. As these ads can be tailored specifically to individual behaviors, users who have searched for gambling-related content might find themselves inundated with enticing offers and promotions.

This hyper-targeted advertising is particularly problematic for those recovering from gambling addiction, as it can exploit psychological vulnerabilities with precision. Therefore, initiatives focusing on advertising restrictions often advocate for clear, conspicuous labels warning about the potential dangers of gambling addiction, much like health warnings on tobacco products.

Community and grassroots efforts have been pivotal in tightening advertising regulations. Advocacy groups often work tirelessly to raise awareness about the impacts of unrestricted gambling ads, lobbying for more stringent policies to protect at-risk populations. Their work highlights the importance of a multi-faceted approach, combining legislative measures with educational campaigns to inform the public about the risks associated with gambling.

Nonetheless, implementing advertising restrictions isn't without challenges. The gambling industry, recognizing advertising as a crucial component of its business model, often pushes back against stringent regulations. Industry stakeholders argue that overly restrictive measures stifle their ability to reach legitimate consumers and impact revenue streams, which can, in turn, affect regulated operations and tax contributions to the economy. This dynamic creates an ongoing debate between industry freedom and public health priorities.

From the psychological viewpoint, advertising plays a significant role in shaping perceptions and attitudes toward gambling. Sophisticated marketing strategies capitalize on the brain's reward system by highlighting the excitement and potential benefits of gambling, exploiting the very mechanisms that psychologists work to understand and counteract. Restricting these messages is a step towards alleviating the societal burden of problem gambling.

In sum, advertising restrictions in gambling serve as a crucial element within the broader spectrum of policy and regulation aimed at combating gambling addiction. As society continues to grapple with the complexities of gambling behaviors, it becomes increasingly important to ensure that advertising practices align with ethical standards that prioritize consumer protection. While regulatory frameworks evolve, the fundamental aim remains constant: to protect individuals from entering the devastating cycle of addiction while maintaining fair play in the gambling industry.

Chapter 19:
Future of Gambling Addiction

As we peer into the future of gambling addiction, it's clear that both the challenges and opportunities will be shaped by the rapid pace of technological advancement. The increasing sophistication of artificial intelligence and machine learning could provide groundbreaking predictive tools for prevention, allowing us to identify those at risk before the addiction takes hold. These developments bring forth a dual-edged sword; while technology could enhance preventive measures and personalize recovery programs, it also adds layers of complexity as new, immersive gambling experiences continue to evolve. Virtual and augmented reality might one day envelop users in hyper-realistic settings, enticing those vulnerable to deeper levels of engagement. The key to fostering healthier gambling habits will lie in a proactive stance—harnessing technology's potential for creating responsible gaming environments while safeguarding individuals from its darker capacities. It's a future where hope lies in adaptability, scientific innovation, and an unwavering commitment to understanding the human psyche. Together, these elements can guide us to a new era of prevention and recovery, providing a beacon of hope for those affected by gambling addiction.

Technological Advances

As we cast our eyes toward the horizon of gambling addiction, technology rises as both a beacon of innovation and a harbinger of potential peril. It weaves itself into the fabric of our lives, reshaping the avenues through which gambling can ensnare the unsuspecting and fortify those striving for liberation. While the landscape of gambling has been evolving for centuries, the rapid pace of technological advances has accelerated the shifts, creating a complex tapestry of challenges and opportunities.

At the forefront of these advances is the proliferation of online platforms that have democratized access to gambling activities. Previously confined to the spaces of brick-and-mortar casinos and betting parlors, gambling can now be accessed from the comfort of one's home or the palm of one's hand. This incredible convenience, coupled with the anonymity online platforms can provide, deepens the potential for addiction. It's a world where digital spins and electronic dice can enthrall vulnerable individuals seeking distraction or thrill in increasingly isolated contexts.

Moreover, the rise of mobile technology has unleashed a new wave of accessibility—betting is no longer an activity confined to scheduled times or dedicated venues. With mobile devices, gambling opportunities are omnipresent. This constant availability can serve as a relentless trigger for individuals battling gambling urges, transforming every idle moment into a potential gateway to addiction. The seamless integration of gambling apps into ubiquitous smartphones blurs the lines between daily life and addictive behavior.

Compounding these challenges is the gamification of non-gambling environments. Many tech-driven platforms employ reward mechanics and interactive designs that mirror traditional gambling, pulling users into cycles of engagement reminiscent of slot machines or poker games. Social media platforms and mobile games integrate features that parallel gambling activities, sometimes encouraging monetary investments for virtual rewards. This slippery slope can inadvertently cultivate the behaviors that underpin gambling addiction in unsuspecting users.

However, with these challenges come promising advances that could offer new pathways to prevention and recovery. One such avenue is the development of predictive tools that harness big data and artificial intelligence. These tools can analyze patterns of behavior, identifying at-risk individuals through their online activities. By spotting the subtle shifts in engagement that precede addiction, these technologies offer hope in intercepting the trajectory towards compulsive gambling before it spirals out of control. Early intervention, facilitated by artificial intelligence, is a promising frontier in the battle against addiction.

Furthermore, technological advances in virtual reality (VR) present unique opportunities for therapeutic interventions. VR can create immersive environments that simulate high-risk situations in a controlled manner, allowing individuals to navigate their responses and develop coping strategies without real-world repercussions. This kind of exposure therapy could be instrumental in desensitizing triggers and reinforcing positive behavioral changes, offering a novel method to aid recovery.

Another technological innovation altering the gambling landscape is blockchain and cryptocurrency. While these technologies contribute to increased anonymity and decentralized betting platforms, potentially complicating regulatory efforts, they also promise greater transparency and fairness in gaming. Smart contracts and decentralized ledgers can ensure that the algorithms behind online gambling are secure and tamper-proof, reducing the potential for manipulation and fostering trust among users.

In parallel, the responsibility of the tech industry grows as these advances unfold. Companies developing gambling environments must prioritize ethical considerations, integrating responsible gaming features into their systems. This could include implementing self-exclusion options, time limits, and spending caps that help users maintain control over their gambling behavior. By leveraging technology to bolster user awareness and control, the industry can contribute to reducing the risk of addiction without stifling innovation.

Education remains a cornerstone in leveraging technology for positive outcomes. Online platforms can be harnessed to disseminate information about the risks of gambling and the signs of addiction. Interactive tools and educational campaigns can raise awareness, empowering potential gamblers with knowledge that may deter them from slipping into addiction. Additionally, digital literacy initiatives can equip users with the critical thinking skills necessary to navigate digital gambling landscapes responsibly.

Looking forward, the technology sector holds the keys to both the proliferation and prevention of gambling addiction. By embracing ethical innovations and proactive measures, the future may hold a balance where technological advances offer protection as much as they offer allure. As society moves into this digital age, it is imperative to harness the immense potential of technology not only to expand the realm of entertainment but also to safeguard those who might falter along its path.

Predictive Tools for Prevention

As our understanding of gambling addiction progresses, so too does our approach to preventing it. A major player on this frontier is the development of predictive tools. These tools aim to identify potential problems before they become entrenched, providing an opportunity for early intervention. With a blend of data analytics, behavioral science, and technology, predictive tools offer a promising strategy in the fight against gambling addiction.

Predictive modeling relies heavily on data—mountains of it. Gambling platforms capture a plethora of user data: frequency of bets, amount wagered, game choices, and even time spent on different activities. Analyzing this information, researchers can begin to discern patterns that may indicate an individual's risk level. It's akin to solving a complex puzzle where each piece of data contributes to a clearer picture of user behavior.

Machine learning algorithms are at the heart of these predictive tools. By processing vast datasets, they can identify subtle behavioral trends and anomalies that would be nearly impossible for humans to detect unaided. These algorithms learn continuously, adapting to new trends and behaviors, thereby improving their predictive accuracy over time. When certain patterns indicative of potential addiction emerge, the system can flag them for further investigation.

How do these tools translate into prevention? The key lies in timely intervention. Once a user is flagged by the predictive model, gambling platforms or mental health professionals can reach out with tailored interventions. This might involve sending automated alerts to suggest a 'cooling-off' period or recommending resources for professional help. The goal is not to police behavior but to offer support and guidance, steering individuals away from potential harm.

For instance, imagine a scenario where an individual starts displaying increased betting behavior late at night, a pattern that's been associated with emotional distress or impulsivity. A predictive model could recognize this early and notify support staff, who might then offer the person resources for financial counseling or emotional support. It's a proactive rather than reactive approach, one that emphasizes care and support.

These predictive tools aren't confined to isolated use. They're often integrated into broader responsible gambling frameworks. Many online platforms now embed these models within their systems, part of a holistic strategy that includes self-exclusion options, limit setting, and enhanced user education about the risks of gambling. The aim is to create an environment that respects user autonomy while promoting healthier interactions with gambling products.

However, the implementation of predictive tools raises several ethical considerations. Concerns about data privacy are paramount. Gambling companies must be transparent about what data they collect and how it's used. Users should have a clear understanding of the predictive systems and access to their own data records. Additionally, the responsibility of ensuring these tools are used ethically lies with both developers and operators, requiring a balance between profit motives and genuine concern for user welfare.

The integration of AI and predictive analytics in gambling raises a tantalizing possibility: could addiction begin to decline thanks to these advances? While the technology is still in its relative infancy, the early results are promising. Some platforms report that interventions based on predictive tools have reduced the incidence of harmful gambling outcomes. Yet, as with any strategy, continuous evaluation and adaptation are crucial.

Behavioral psychology also plays an integral role in refining these tools. Understanding why people gamble and the triggers that escalate their behavior is essential for improving the algorithms. Insights from psychology help ensure that models don't just react to raw data but consider the human stories behind the numbers. This holistic approach combines technological and human insights, maximizing the potential for meaningful prevention strategies.

There's an optimistic horizon for those concerned with gambling addiction. As predictive tools develop, they hold the potential to transform how society approaches prevention. More personalized, data-driven interventions could mean that individuals receive help before manifesting clear symptoms of addiction. This forward-thinking method champions the belief that prevention isn't just possible; it's actionable and within reach.

In a future where technology shapes our understanding of human behavior, predictive tools stand as beacons of hope. They embody the potential to sidestep the pitfalls of addiction before they take hold, offering a pathway to healthier habits and ultimately, a brighter future for those vulnerable to the allure of gambling. With continued refinement and ethical application, these tools could reshape not just individual lives but societal norms surrounding gambling and addiction prevention.

Chapter 20:
Personal Stories of Recovery

In this chapter, we dive into the compelling personal narratives of those who have fought and triumphed over gambling addiction. Each story is a beacon of hope, shedding light on the transformative journey from the depths of despair to the heights of personal victory. These individuals lay bare their struggles and triumphs, illustrating that the road to recovery is uniquely personal, yet universally inspiring. Their tales are peppered with moments of revelation—those small turning points that illuminate the path forward. From encountering profound cultural shifts to the quiet strength found in therapeutic support, these success narratives offer invaluable lessons not only in resilience but in the profound human capacity for change. As you read these stories, you'll discover insights and strategies that underscore the possibility of reclaiming life from the clutches of addiction, reaffirming the belief that recovery is not just a destination but a rewarding journey of rediscovery.

Success Narratives

Success narratives in the realm of gambling recovery offer more than just a ray of hope; they serve as living testaments to the resilience and strength inherent in those who choose to confront their addiction. These stories form a mosaic of human tenacity and transformation, illustrating that change is possible, no matter how deep the abyss might seem. Each story is unique, showcasing different paths and strategies that have enabled individuals to regain control over their lives. Through these accounts, we can glean valuable lessons on perseverance, courage, and the innovative strategies that have proven effective in overcoming the grips of gambling addiction.

Tony's journey is one such narrative. He was a high-stakes poker player whose life spiraled into chaos when winning became his singular focus. At the height of his addiction, he stumbled into considerable debt, jeopardizing not just his financial well-being, but also his family relationships. It wasn't until he saw his daughter's disappointment on her birthday, when he couldn't afford her much-desired gift, that the weight of his addiction truly sank in. This moment became a pivotal point in his life. Tony sought help through therapy, joined a gambling support group, and most importantly, redefined his understanding of what winning truly meant. Today, Tony channels his passion for poker into teaching strategy sessions that focus on mathematical skills, steering clear of emotional traps. His story is a vivid reminder of the personal transformations that can occur when one embraces the difficult but rewarding path to recovery.

There is power in peer stories, and Jane's story further embodies this. She spent years wrapped in the glitz of slot machines, convinced that the next spin would change her luck. After hitting rock bottom, Jane decided to attend a group therapy session, initially driven by her partner's insistence. She wasn't seeking help; she was proving a point that she didn't need assistance. However, as she listened to the stories of others who found themselves in similar situations, a sense of belonging and understanding began to change her perspective. She discovered that her own experiences could not only aid her recovery but also help others. Jane became an active participant and later an advocate, sharing her experiences on public platforms to spread awareness. Her narrative underlines the transformative power of community support and the role empathy plays in fostering recovery.

Then there's Alex, whose story shines a light on the harrowing experience of gambling addiction paired with another form of mental illness. Diagnosed with depression, Alex found himself caught in the web of gambling as a form of escape, each bet a feeble attempt to momentarily lift the emotional burden. It was during a particularly desperate period that Alex hit a low so profound it necessitated immediate intervention. Enrolling in a dual-diagnosis treatment center, Alex began the arduous journey of tackling both his depression and gambling addiction concurrently. The integration of Cognitive Behavioral Therapy with medication management proved vital. By reprogramming his thought patterns, Alex re-learned how to manage stress and find joy in non-gambling-related activities. In the end, Alex's account highlights the importance of addressing co-occurring disorders for a successful recovery journey.

These success narratives remind us that recovery is not linear. The path is filled with obstacles, potential pitfalls, and continuous self-discovery. An essential element across all these stories is the recognition of the need for help. Whether it is reaching out to friends, family, or professional services, the realization that one does not have to navigate recovery alone can be empowering. Importantly, these narratives emphasize adaptability; what works for one individual might not work for another. Flexibility in strategies—whether it be behavioral therapy, family support, or self-help groups—remains crucial as each person's journey is as unique as their fingerprint.

The story of Maria enhances our understanding of varied international contexts and cultural nuances in recovery. Growing up in an environment where gambling was a celebrated social activity, Maria found herself caught between cultural expectations and her increasing dependence on the thrill of betting. It was only by exploring her cultural background and its influence on her behavior that Maria devised a strategy for recovery that resonated with her personal experience. Her narrative is a testament to the necessity of culturally sensitive approaches in crafting effective recovery plans.

Michael's success narrative draws attention to the often-overlooked role of financial counseling in the recovery process. His gambling addiction led him to a financial crisis, making the road to recovery seem daunting. However, by working closely with a financial counselor, Michael not only learned to manage his debts but also reestablished his trust with family members. His journey underscores how addressing financial recovery alongside psychological healing can significantly bolster one's path to a gambling-free life.

Among these success stories, the overriding theme is resilience. Each person had to confront their addiction, accept its impact on their lives, and make conscious choices for change. The power of these narratives lies in their honesty and their message that recovery, though challenging, is very much attainable. They serve as beacons for anyone who finds themselves lost in the turmoil of gambling addiction, proving that while the journey is hard, the destination—reconnection with life and loved ones—is well worth the struggle.

These narratives are not just chapters in a book; they are living testimonies, urging readers to look beyond statistics and see the human faces behind the numbers. They implore us to consider recovery as a dynamic and ongoing commitment to personal growth and change. By uplifting these voices, we can nourish hope, foster community, and perhaps inspire more triumphs on the road to recovery.

Lessons Learned

Through the personal stories of recovery, one theme reverberates with profound clarity: the journey to overcome gambling addiction is as unique as the individuals undertaking it. No single path encompasses every experience, yet common threads weave through each narrative, offering insights and hope. The first lesson learned is the critical importance of self-awareness. In countless stories, the turning point came when individuals finally acknowledged the depth of their addiction. It wasn't just about recognizing a problem; it was about understanding its roots, triggers, and influence. This realization, though sometimes painful, was liberating, transforming acknowledgment into action.

Another crucial lesson is the immense power of support systems. Many individuals recount moments when a friend's persistent encouragement or a family's unwavering belief made all the difference. Recovery isn't a solitary endeavor. It thrives on connection, empathy, and shared strength. Support groups, whether formal or informal, play a pivotal role, providing a space where people can share experiences without judgment. For many, the camaraderie found in group settings reaffirms that they are not alone. This collective empathy builds a foundation of resilience, offering hope that change is possible when supported by others who understand.

Moreover, stories of recovery highlight a significant insight: setbacks are not failures. They're an inherent part of the process. The narratives suggest that relapse can be an opportunity for growth rather than a regression. Such experiences teach individuals to identify weaknesses and fortify their defenses. Thus, resilience isn't merely about enduring hardship but about learning, adapting, and forging ahead with renewed determination. This attitude requires a shift in perspective, where setbacks serve as stepping stones rather than stumbling blocks on the path to recovery.

Another lesson emphasized is the dynamic nature of recovery strategies. What works for one person may not work for another. Individuals describe the trial-and-error process they underwent to discover the blend of therapies, activities, and lifestyle changes that suited them best. Some found solace in mindfulness and meditation, while others benefited from volunteering or engaging in creative pursuits. Such diversity in approaches demonstrates that recovery must be personalized, allowing individuals to reclaim aspects of their identity that gambling had overshadowed.

The stories also illuminate the transformative power of purpose. Many recovering individuals found that having a goal—be it a new career, a hobby, or reconnecting with family—gave their recovery a focal point and imbued their efforts with meaning. Purposeful pursuits helped fill the void that gambling once occupied, providing structure and motivation to continue on the path to healing. This aligned purpose often became the anchor that kept them steady amidst life's inherent turbulences.

An important realization is the impact of addressing underlying emotional issues that fueled the addiction. Numerous narratives mention the struggles with anxiety, depression, or past trauma that coexisted with their gambling habits. Tackling these issues head-on through therapy and counseling not only aided in recovery but also equipped individuals with healthier coping mechanisms. This holistic approach underscores the necessity of treating the whole person, rather than merely focusing on the symptoms of addiction.

Financial education and management emerge as vital elements in the stories shared. For many, gambling was an escape from financial stress, yet ironically exacerbated their monetary woes. Learning to budget, manage debt, and establish financial goals became a therapeutic part of the recovery process. Through practical skills and newfound financial literacy, individuals gained confidence, leading to greater independence and a reduced urge to gamble as a quick fix.

Perhaps the most uplifting lesson is the realization of one's potential to inspire and help others. As individuals journey through recovery, many discover that their stories can be powerful tools for advocacy and support. Sharing experiences provides hope to those still struggling, creating a ripple effect that extends beyond personal recovery. This empowerment instills a sense of community and responsibility, reminding individuals that overcoming addiction isn't merely an end goal but a continuous process of growth and contribution.

Finally, the stories collectively emphasize the notion of reclaiming one's narrative. Gambling once dictated much of their lives, but recovery is about taking back control. It's about rewriting the story, where choices are made not from a place of compulsion but from a place of clarity and intention. This reclamation is empowering, instilling a sense of agency that gambling once stole. Individuals learned to define themselves not by their past but by their strength to rise above it.

The journey of recovery, as depicted in these personal stories, is complex, multifaceted, and deeply human. Each lesson learned contributes to a broader understanding of overcoming gambling addiction, offering inspiration, strategies, and hope for those navigating their path. In the end, it's a testament to the resilience of the human spirit, the healing power of connection, and the limitless potential for change.

Chapter 21:
Debunking Myths

Dispelling myths surrounding gambling addiction is crucial for understanding its true nature and overcoming societal misconceptions. Many believe that gambling addiction stems solely from a lack of willpower or moral failing, yet scientific studies unravel a more intricate picture. Individuals facing gambling addiction often grapple with complex interactions between genetic predispositions, environmental influences, and neural mechanisms that transcend mere vise or choice. It's akin to the myth of Sisyphus, where the struggle itself becomes a looming shadow rather than the mountain's summit. Some misconceptions suggest that all gamblers are reckless or financially irresponsible; however, understanding that the addiction is often an emotional response to unmet psychological needs can transform our perception. Recognizing these myths enables a compassionate, informed approach towards prevention and recovery, dismantling stigmas and fostering healing environments. In separating fact from fiction, we establish a foundation for progressive strategies that embrace empathy and evidence-based interventions, crafting pathways not only for individual redemption but for societal understanding as well.

Common Misconceptions

In the complex world of gambling addiction, misconceptions abound. These misunderstandings can obscure the reality of addiction, making it harder for individuals to seek help or for society to tackle the issue effectively. One common misbelief is that gambling addiction solely stems from a lack of willpower. People often equate it with personal weakness, thinking that those affected could simply choose to stop if they wanted to. However, research reveals that gambling addiction is a deeply entrenched psychological issue, influenced by various factors such as brain chemistry, environment, and even genetics.

Another widespread misconception is that only certain types of games lead to addiction. While high-stakes poker or slot machines are often identified as culprits, the truth is that any form of gambling can become addictive, depending on the individual's psychological and emotional state. It's not the game itself but the person's relationship with it that defines the risk of addiction. The illusion of control—a common phenomenon where gamblers believe they can influence the outcome of a game of chance—further fuels this trap. It's crucial to understand that the lure of any game can be dangerously compelling under the right circumstances.

Many also believe that gambling addiction is less harmful than substance abuse because it doesn't involve ingesting harmful substances. This misconception undermines the severe impact that gambling can have on a person's mental health, relationships, and financial stability. The compulsive behavior associated with gambling addiction triggers intense emotional distress, anxiety, and depression. Financial ruin often follows, leading to stress and despair both for the person battling the addiction and their loved ones. In some cases, the psychological pain can be similar to or even exceed that experienced by individuals addicted to substances.

The social stigma surrounding gambling addiction also perpetuates myths. Often, society views gambling as a harmless pastime or a rite of passage rather than a potential life-ruining problem. This perception can pressure individuals to partake in gambling activities, dismissing their significant consequences. It also discourages people with gambling problems from admitting they have an issue and seeking treatment. The fear of being judged or seen as incapable can prevent many from taking the first crucial steps towards recovery. Recognizing gambling as a legitimate mental health issue is vital in breaking down these social barriers.

One intriguing but false belief is that gambling can be a valid way to make a living. The portrayal of professional gamblers living glamorous lifestyles promotes the idea that gambling can be a consistent and respectable source of income. This misconception ignores the reality that for the majority, gambling is a high-risk endeavor that results in financial loss rather than gain. While stories of big wins are often sensationalized, the truth is that casinos and gambling institutions are designed to profit more than the players. Seemingly glamorous success stories obscure the hard truth of the severe financial and emotional consequences faced by many.

Another dangerous myth is that those who are addicted must continually gamble themselves into financial destruction. Some individuals are capable of maintaining their addiction to a certain threshold without reaching financial ruin. However, this doesn't make their addiction any less severe. The emotional void and the underlying psychological issues persist, affecting other aspects of their lives such as personal relationships and career. Understanding that gambling addiction isn't solely about visible damage like debt helps in acknowledging the hidden scars it leaves on one's mental and emotional health.

Moreover, it's a misconception that individuals can outgrow gambling addiction without any assistance. The "phase" argument suggests that some people simply move past gambling as they mature or after a lucky break. However, addiction doesn't resolve without effort and often requires professional help to address both the visible behaviors and the underlying psychological dependencies. Recovery is a journey that involves understanding triggers and cultivating healthier coping mechanisms rather than relying on the notion of outgrowing the addiction.

Lastly, there's an assumption that technologies like online gambling apps or mobile betting only attract the younger generations. Contrary to this belief, technology can appeal to gamblers of all ages, offering accessibility that caters to varied preferences and habits. The ease of access and the anonymity provided by digital platforms can entice older generations as well, contributing to gambling behaviors across age groups. Recognizing this technological impact is integral to combating the spread of gambling addiction among diverse demographics.

Separating Fact from Fiction

In the landscape of gambling addiction, myths and misconceptions abound, clouding judgment and often skewing public perception. These misunderstandings can significantly impact those seeking help or those who might not even recognize they need it. Let's untangle some of these fallacies, paving the way for a clearer, more compassionate understanding of this complex issue.

One of the most enduring myths is the belief that gambling addiction is simply a lack of willpower. This misconception can be particularly damaging, as it not only stigmatizes those suffering but also deters them from seeking help out of shame or fear of judgment. Research consistently shows that addiction is a multifaceted issue, deeply rooted in psychological and biological factors. It's not merely about "bad choices" or moral failings, but rather an interplay of genetic predispositions, neurological imbalances, and environmental triggers.

This myth that one can just "snap out of it" implies that healing from gambling addiction is straightforward or self-managed. In reality, recovery is a journey that often requires professional guidance, support systems, and sometimes medical intervention. It's a process that demands patience, understanding, and a variety of therapeutic strategies to address the underlying causes and rebuild one's life.

Another common fiction is the assumption that only those with a specific type of personality can become addicted. Often, people imagine a stereotype: the high-roller, the risk-taker, or someone with a flamboyant lifestyle. While it is true that certain personality traits can increase the likelihood of engaging in risky behaviors, gambling addiction is an equal-opportunity affliction. It cuts across all demographics, affecting people from all walks of life, including those who might not typically engage in high-risk activities.

The impact of stress and emotional instability is frequently overlooked as a contributing factor in gambling addiction. Many become entrapped in the cycle of gambling not only because of the thrill or potential financial gain but also as an escape mechanism from emotional pain or life stressors. It is crucial to recognize the emotional triggers that often underpin compulsive gambling behaviors. Acknowledging this sheds light on the importance of addressing emotional well-being as part of comprehensive addiction treatment.

One myth that lulls people into a false sense of security is the belief in the "big win" as a solution to financial woes. This fallacy perpetuates the idea that gambling can be a reasonable strategy for resolving money problems. Instead of alleviating financial stressors, it invariably exacerbates them. The allure of the big win triggers a cycle of chasing losses, leading to mounting debt and further desperation.

An important distinction must also be made between gambling for recreation and gambling addiction. While casual gambling can indeed exist, characterized by entertainment and social interaction with no detrimental effects, the line between enjoyment and pathology can become blurred. It's vital to discern when recreational activities veer into harmful patterns, influenced by frequency, the amount of money spent, and the emotional dependency on the activity.

Another pervasive myth surrounds the idea that gambling addiction is less dangerous than substance abuse. Often seen as a socially acceptable activity—even glamorized—the harmful effects are underestimated. Yet, the psychological and financial devastation caused by addiction can be just as ruinous as any chemical dependency. The impulsivity, changes in behavior, and even physical health consequences mirror those found in other forms of addiction.

There's also a myth that online gambling is safer because it lacks the traditional casino setting, but in reality, it's more insidious. The anonymity and accessibility of online platforms can accelerate the addiction process. With fewer social controls than visiting physical locations, individuals can indulge in secret, often unnoticed until significant damage has occurred.

A hopeful myth is the belief that those who recognize their gambling problem can easily find help and recover on their own. Unfortunately, the path to recovery is often punctuated by denial and relapse. Understanding that treatment is typically complex and long-term is essential. It may include therapy, support groups, medication, and lifestyle changes, all tailored to the individual's unique circumstances.

Finally, it's vital to address the misconception that once someone achieves sobriety from gambling, the risk of relapse is minimal. In truth, continuous vigilance is necessary, with high awareness of triggers and preventive strategies to maintain recovery. Recovery from gambling addiction is ongoing, similar to managing other forms of compulsions, requiring an enduring commitment to personal well-being and support.

By separating fact from fiction, we empower individuals with knowledge, fostering empathy and eliminating barriers to seeking help. Dispelling myths not only opens avenues for effective intervention but also nurtures an environment where recovery is celebrated and shame is eradicated. Understanding the true nature of gambling addiction is crucial for creating supportive communities where individuals feel safe to come forward, seek help, and eventually, reclaim their lives.

Chapter 22:
Research and Insights

In the constantly evolving field of gambling addiction, recent research illuminates a spectrum of insights that refine our understanding of this complex behavior. Groundbreaking studies delve into the intricate interplay between neurological pathways, environmental triggers, and individual vulnerabilities, revealing a mosaic of factors that contribute to addiction. This wealth of data not only uncovers the underlying psychological mechanisms but also paves the way for future innovations in treatment and prevention. As researchers scrutinize emerging patterns, notably influenced by technology and societal shifts, they're opening doors to fascinating possibilities for more effective interventions. These insights inspire hope for creating tailored strategies that address the nuanced needs of diverse populations, potentially heralding a new era in combating gambling addiction where knowledge translates into empowerment and recovery. With each study, the path forward becomes clearer, encouraging those impacted by addiction to believe in the possibility of change and a healthier future.

Recent Studies

In recent years, research into gambling addiction has gained significant momentum, shedding light on previously uncharted territories of the human psyche. The quest to understand why certain individuals become entrapped by the lure of gambling, while others can partake without consequence, has led to a surge in scientific studies. These studies are diligently probing the neurological, psychological, and social factors that contribute to gambling addiction, offering fresh insights and guiding the development of more effective prevention and treatment strategies.

A salient theme that has emerged from these recent studies is the understanding of gambling addiction as a complex interplay of genetic, environmental, and psychological factors. Much like other behavioral addictions, gambling doesn't stem from a single source but rather from a constellation of influences. A study published in *Addiction Biology* illustrated that genetic predispositions might play a role in how individuals respond to risk and rewards. Interestingly, the study found certain gene variants that are associated with a heightened risk of developing gambling addiction, similar to those linked to substance abuse disorders.

Beyond genetic factors, the neurological underpinnings of gambling addiction are being mapped with increasing precision. Advances in brain imaging technologies have enhanced our understanding of how the reward circuitry in the brain drives compulsive gambling behaviors. These studies often focus on the role of dopamine, a neurotransmitter renowned for its role in reward, pleasure, and motivation. A groundbreaking study from the University of Cambridge used functional MRI scans to observe how the brains of gambling addicts respond to monetary rewards and losses. The findings revealed an overactive reward system similar to that seen in cocaine addicts, thereby cementing gambling addiction's standing as a brain disorder.

Alongside neurological research, there has been a surge in psychological studies aimed at uncovering the cognitive distortions that fuel gambling behaviors. Research has shown that individuals addicted to gambling often possess a distorted understanding of probability and chance, leading to what experts call "cognitive fallacies." For instance, a common fallacy is the "illusion of control," where gamblers believe they can influence the outcome of a game of chance. Recent studies indicate that these cognitive distortions are not simply byproducts of gambling but are deeply embedded in the cognitive processes of affected individuals. Understanding these distortions is crucial, as they are not only central to the development of addiction but also to its maintenance over time.

Research is also exploring the sociocultural factors that contribute to the prevalence and character of gambling addiction. Certain studies have investigated how cultural attitudes towards gambling can influence individual behaviors. For example, research conducted across different cultural settings has shown that environments where gambling is viewed as an acceptable and normal leisure activity tend to have higher rates of addiction. These findings underscore the importance of cultural context in understanding and addressing the roots of gambling addiction.

Moreover, the impact of technology and accessibility on gambling habits has not been overlooked in recent research. With the rapid growth of online casinos and mobile betting apps, studies are investigating how these technologies have changed the landscape of gambling—and addiction. Research published in the *Journal of Behavioral Addictions* highlights the alarming ease with which individuals can access gambling platforms from virtually anywhere, at any time. This omnipresent accessibility often leads to increased frequency and duration of gambling sessions, exacerbating addiction risks.

An often-overlooked area in gambling research is the psychological and emotional triggers that lead individuals to start and continue gambling. Recent studies emphasize the role of negative emotional states, such as anxiety and depression, in gambling addiction. Many individuals use gambling as a form of escape, a way to temporarily alleviate emotional pain. A study in the *American Journal on Addictions* found that individuals with higher levels of stress and emotional distress were more likely to engage in problematic gambling, highlighting the need for mental health interventions as part of comprehensive treatment plans.

The latest studies are also tackling the critical issue of detection and early intervention. New tools and methodologies are being developed to identify at-risk individuals before they develop full-blown gambling addiction. Some recent research is focused on predictive analytics and machine learning models that can analyze betting patterns to flag potential problems. By leveraging big data, these studies aim to create algorithms that identify risky behaviors early on, allowing for timely intervention and support.

A particularly innovative area of research looks at the efficacy of various therapeutic interventions. Cognitive-behavioral therapy (CBT) has long been established as an effective treatment for gambling addiction, but recent studies seek to refine and optimize these approaches. A study published in *Clinical Psychology Review* suggests that customizing CBT to address individual cognitive distortions and emotional triggers can significantly improve treatment outcomes. Moreover, there is growing interest in integrating mindfulness-based interventions to help individuals manage cravings and develop healthier coping mechanisms.

An exciting development in gambling addiction research is the examination of peer support networks and their role in recovery. Studies have shown that involvement in peer support groups can provide valuable social reinforcement, reducing feelings of isolation and promoting sustained recovery. Research published in the *Journal of Group Dynamics* indicates that individuals who actively participate in group support sessions often report higher levels of satisfaction and motivation in their recovery journeys.

These recent studies collectively offer a tapestry of insights into the multifaceted nature of gambling addiction. From understanding its genetic roots and neurological pathways to exploring psychological, cultural, and technological influences, researchers are forming a more complete picture of why addiction occurs and how it might be prevented and treated. As these investigations continue to unravel the complexities of gambling addiction, they pave the way for more effective strategies to help individuals break free from its grips and lead healthier, more fulfilling lives.

Future Directions

Exploring the frontiers of gambling addiction research is a journey into a complex labyrinth, one where emerging technologies and innovative methodologies promise to reshape our understanding of this intricate phenomenon. As we stand on the cusp of new discoveries, the role of the digital age cannot be overstated. With the proliferation of online platforms and the advent of artificial intelligence, future research is poised to delve deeper into the intricacies of addiction behaviors shaped and exacerbated by technological influences.

One promising direction lies in the development of predictive tools utilizing machine learning algorithms. By analyzing vast quantities of user data, researchers can gain insights into the early indicators of gambling addiction, potentially identifying at-risk individuals before they spiral into more severe patterns of behavior. These predictive models could revolutionize prevention strategies, offering targeted interventions that are both timely and effective.

Moreover, breakthroughs in neuroscience continue to illuminate the pathways that underpin addictive behaviors. The integration of neuroimaging technologies, such as fMRI and PET scans, provides a window into the brain's reward system in real time. This allows researchers to observe how neural mechanisms respond to gambling stimuli, thereby uncovering the biological underpinnings that drive compulsive gambling.

Future research is also likely to focus on personalized intervention strategies. While current therapeutic approaches often adopt a one-size-fits-all model, advancements in genomics might offer personalized treatment plans that take an individual's genetic predispositions into account. This tailored approach could enhance the effectiveness of recovery programs by aligning them more closely with an individual's unique biological and psychological profile.

The environment where gambling takes place is rapidly evolving, too. Virtual reality (VR) and augmented reality (AR) are not just transforming gaming experiences; they present novel challenges and opportunities for addiction research. Understanding how these immersive technologies affect the perception of risk and reward could open new avenues for both harm reduction and therapeutic applications.

On a broader scale, interdisciplinary research will become increasingly vital. Collaboration among psychologists, neuroscientists, data analysts, and policymakers will be essential to address the multifaceted nature of gambling addiction. This cross-pollination of ideas could lead to the formulation of comprehensive strategies that integrate insights from diverse fields, ultimately producing more holistic solutions.

Ethical considerations will also come to the forefront of future studies. As surveillance technologies advance, balancing the potential for monitoring at-risk behavior with the necessity of safeguarding privacy rights remains a delicate challenge. Researchers and practitioners will need to navigate these ethical waters carefully, ensuring that interventions are not only effective but also respectful of individual freedoms.

In addition, the global nature of gambling necessitates an understanding of cultural contexts. Future research might focus on how cultural norms and values influence gambling behaviors across different societies, providing insights that can tailor prevention and intervention strategies to be culturally sensitive and effective.

Finally, engagement with the public will become an essential component of future directions. Increasing awareness and education around the risks of gambling addiction, along with promoting supportive community networks, can serve as protective factors against the tide of this growing concern. Advocacy and grassroots movements will play a crucial role in shaping public policy and societal attitudes towards gambling.

As the landscape of gambling continues to transform, so too must our approaches to understanding and mitigating its impacts. The journey ahead is one of collaboration, innovation, and ethically grounded research, promising a future where gambling addiction is both better understood and more effectively contained.

Chapter 23:
Ethical Considerations

In exploring the ethical considerations surrounding gambling addiction, it's crucial to navigate the moral and societal responsibilities that accompany this complex issue. The tension between individual freedom and societal protection raises challenging questions: at what point does personal choice transition into harmful compulsion, and when should regulatory bodies step in? The gambling industry, driven by profit yet carrying the weight of responsibility, finds itself at a crossroads where ethical duty must balance with economic interests. Transparency, informed consent, and corporate accountability become pivotal in ensuring that vulnerable individuals are not exploited. As the industry continues to innovate, the ethical landscape demands that technology, too, serves to protect rather than prey. It's a call not just for policy-makers and business leaders, but for society as a whole, to foster an environment where recovery and prevention are prioritized, affirming the dignity and autonomy of those battling addiction.

Moral Dilemmas

The realm of gambling unfolds many moral dilemmas, where the line between personal responsibility and societal accountability is often blurred. At the core of these dilemmas is the question of agency. When does an individual's choice to gamble morph into a struggle with addiction that requires intervention? This question is not just about understanding the psychological mechanisms but also assessing the ethical landscape surrounding autonomy and dependency.

Consider the argument of free will, the age-old debate that stretches beyond gambling back into philosophical discourse. At what point do external factors—such as enticing casino environments or ubiquitous online betting platforms—diminish an individual's freedom to choose? It's essential to explore how much the design of gambling products influences behavior versus how much responsibility rests on the individual. This framing is often central to discussions about responsibility, impacting not only those struggling with addiction but also influencing public policy and regulatory frameworks.

Adding complexity to this moral quagmire is the portrayal of gambling as a harmless entertainment activity. While it can provide enjoyment and a social outlet for many, for others, it represents a path to ruin. This duality raises ethical concerns on how gambling is marketed and portrayed in media. Should the responsibility of messaging fall squarely on the shoulders of the industry, or is it a shared one with governments and society? Crafting balanced narratives becomes paramount, not only to protect the vulnerable but also to respect the rights of those who engage in gambling recreationally.

One major moral dilemma is the responsibility of the gambling industry itself. The industry's profit motive often conflicts with its ethical duty to safeguard players against addiction. Should gambling companies implement stringent measures to prevent addiction, even if it diminishes their profits? The implementation and effectiveness of self-exclusion programs and the use of technology to identify problem gambling behaviors are significant ethical discussions within this realm. The spectrum of industry responsibility stretches from token gestures to robust, effective intervention systems.

Furthermore, the question of informed consent surfaces frequently in conversations about gambling ethics. Do individuals truly understand the risks involved when gambling? In a world where the intricacies of odds and probabilities are deliberately masked or obscured by lavish advertising and optimistic narratives, the notion of informed consent seems, at times, more theoretical than practical. Providing gamblers with transparent information is an ethical requirement that cannot be overlooked, serving as a counterbalance to the psychological lures that hook players into spending beyond their means.

On a societal level, the economic benefits reaped from gambling taxes present a moral contradiction. Governments often rely on revenue from gambling while also bearing the social costs associated with addiction. This financial dependency raises ethical questions about the extent to which public policies are influenced by economic benefits rather than the wellbeing of citizens. Striking a balance between profiting from gambling and protecting public health is a difficult yet necessary endeavor, calling for transparent governance and ethical diligence.

Additionally, the accessibility of gambling technologies introduces another ethical conundrum. The advent of online and mobile betting has made gambling more accessible than ever, breaking down geographical and physical barriers. Ethical considerations must address how such accessibility can exacerbate addiction, particularly among youth and other vulnerable populations. Is it morally justifiable to capitalize on technological advances that make it easier for people to gamble from the privacy of their homes, or should there be stronger regulatory oversight to prevent potential harm?

Family dynamics bring a further layer of complexity to the ethical discourse surrounding gambling. The impact of an individual's gambling behavior often extends beyond themselves, affecting partners, children, and broader family units. What ethical considerations arise in situations where a family's financial stability is jeopardized by one member's addiction? The moral obligation of family members to intervene, coupled with the emotional weight of such situations, presents an intricate tapestry of ethical and emotional challenges.

Beyond personal and familial spheres, gambling also has broader societal impacts. Communities with high rates of gambling addiction frequently struggle with associated issues such as crime and financial instability. Addressing these ethical concerns involves evaluating the role of community support networks and the responsibilities of local governments in providing services and resources to mitigate these effects.

Lastly, we must consider the ethical obligations toward individuals who have recovered from gambling addiction. They often face stigma and limited support systems as they reintegrate into society. Ensuring dignity, respect, and opportunities for these individuals are upheld is one of the ethical challenges that society faces, encouraging a paradigm shift toward healing and understanding rather than judgment and exclusion.

In unpacking these moral dilemmas, it becomes clear that they are woven into the very fabric of human choice, societal values, and economic imperatives. Navigating them requires continuous dialogue among stakeholders, balancing compassion with accountability, and fostering policies that are as informed by ethics as they are by economics. Understanding these dilemmas is an ongoing journey that brings to light the dual nature of gambling as both a source of enjoyment and a potential pathway to suffering.

Industry Responsibilities

The gambling industry stands at a pivotal crossroads where ethical responsibility and commercial interests intersect. As it continues to evolve, particularly with the rise of digital and mobile gambling, the industry's responsibilities grow proportionally more complex. The ethical considerations that the industry must grapple with go beyond merely obeying existing regulations. They extend to the very heart of how gambling operators design their games, advertise their services, and support their clientele who might be at risk of developing addiction issues.

The sheer allure and accessibility of gambling have been amplified by sophisticated marketing strategies and user-friendly platforms. These elements beckon consumers, drawing them into cycles of anticipation and reward. Herein lies a significant responsibility for the industry: to ensure that its marketing does not exploit vulnerable individuals. Advertisements should not promote gambling as a solution to financial troubles or portray it as risk-free fun. Instead, the industry ought to present balanced messages that highlight the potential risks alongside the rewards, thus providing a comprehensive picture to the consumer.

Disclosures about odds, potential losses, and the nature of chance should be transparent and prominent. When a gambler logs onto a platform, they should easily find information delineating the realities of gambling, instead of being tugged by the flashy promises of jackpots. It's here that user education becomes a cornerstone of industry responsibility. Operators should leverage their platforms to educate users, integrating educational tools that explain risk, probability, and the potential for addiction.

Progress must also be made in terms of game design. The way a game is structured can either minimize or exacerbate the risk of addiction. Thoughtful and ethical design decisions are crucial. The mechanics of these games, such as reward schedules, should be scrutinized to avoid reinforcing addictive behaviors. While the excitement of winning is integral to gambling, creating environments that foster responsible play and offering options to set personal limits could greatly aid in mitigating excessive risk-taking behavior.

Initiatives for self-exclusion are steps in the right direction. However, the industry should escalate efforts in making these options more proactive and accessible. In an ideal setup, gamblers should have easy access to tools that allow them to regulate their gambling activities. Features such as wagering limits, time-outs, and self-assessment tools should be standard offerings across all platforms. These mechanisms empower users to retain a degree of control over their gambling habits, potentially preventing problematic behavior before it flourishes into full-blown addiction.

Furthermore, providing robust support systems is an ethical obligation that cannot be overlooked. Gambling operators have the resources to contribute significantly to research and treatment of gambling addiction. Supporting initiatives dedicated to understanding the psychological and behavioral underpinnings of gambling addiction enhances both prevention and treatment efforts. By investing in these areas, the industry not only demonstrates social responsibility but also actively participates in the broader discourse on public health and addiction.

Collaborations with researchers and healthcare professionals can foster an environment of accountability. Such partnerships can lead to innovative strategies and policies that prioritize consumer welfare over profit maximization. *Engagement with stakeholders* who are dedicated to understanding and combating gambling addiction can identify best practices and outline practical ways the industry can align its interests with those that safeguard player welfare.

This extends to responsible data usage as well. The gambling industry possesses enormous amounts of user data, and it's their responsibility to utilize this data ethically. By employing predictive analytics, operators can identify patterns indicative of problem gambling, allowing them to intervene before these patterns evolve into detrimental behavior. Notification systems could be designed to alert players who exhibit signs of distress, encouraging them to seek support. In essence, this data should be harnessed not just for profit but for active, responsible gaming oversight.

Industry responsibility also reflects in the support for comprehensive public policy and smart regulation. By advocating for policies that protect all stakeholders, the industry can demonstrate that it prioritizes player safety over short-term financial gain. Supporting legislation that imposes limits on advertising targeted at vulnerable populations, as well as backing age verification systems, aligns with ethical imperatives aimed at reducing harm.

Moreover, the industry's role includes initiating conversations that lead to cultural shifts in how gambling is perceived and engaged with. Industry leaders can exert influence by promoting a culture where gambling is recognized as an activity that carries inherent risks, fostering an environment where seeking help is normalized, rather than stigmatized. This means actively participating in and funding public awareness campaigns that communicate the realities of gambling.

Ultimately, the industry must continually reassess its practices and remain open to change. As the understanding of gambling addiction progresses, and as new technological platforms emerge, companies need to be at the forefront of adopting ethical standards that are attuned to these advancements. This is not just a forethought but a continuous commitment that requires vigilance, creativity, and a genuine concern for the well-being of consumers.

The challenges are substantial, yet the possibilities for impactful change are equally significant. By embracing their responsibilities, gambling operators have the opportunity to lead with integrity, setting a standard for other consumer industries to follow. This is not just about fulfilling a philanthropic duty; it's about reshaping the landscape of the gambling world itself. Ethical stewardship promises not only sustainable business practices but also a healthier, more informed player base.

Chapter 24:
Community Resources

Understanding and addressing gambling addiction is not a journey undertaken alone; it requires the strength of a community and the availability of robust resources to guide individuals and their families along the path to recovery. Across diverse locales, community programs and support networks provide the essential scaffolding for those seeking to break free from the grip of gambling addiction. Whether through local support groups that offer a safe haven for sharing experiences, or national helplines that connect individuals with immediate assistance, these resources empower the afflicted to regain control and start anew. Building a network of understanding within one's community not only facilitates personal recovery but also fosters an environment where awareness and empathy can thrive, mitigating stigma and encouraging more proactive approaches to prevention and support. The journey to recovery is strengthened by communal empathy and action, creating a tapestry of resilience that uplifts individuals and fortifies collective efforts against the perils of addiction.

Finding Help

Realizing the need for help with gambling addiction can feel overwhelming yet liberating. Those grappling with this compulsion often find themselves trapped in a cycle of denial and justification, where the line between enjoyment and addiction blurs. Admitting that help is necessary is an essential first step towards recovery. But what does finding help look like in practice?

The landscape of community resources available for gambling addiction is broad and diverse. From non-profit organizations to governmental agencies, the support available can provide a lifeline for individuals seeking to regain control of their lives. One of the critical aspects of finding help is understanding that it often requires a multi-pronged approach. This might include counseling services, financial advice, and community groups that offer both emotional and social support.

Local community centers and health services often have programs tailored to address gambling addiction. These programs typically involve trained professionals who understand the intricacies of gambling behavior and can offer personalized support. Counselors and therapists who specialize in addiction treatment can provide the tools needed to address the underlying psychological triggers that fuel gambling urges. Moreover, these professionals can work with individuals to develop coping strategies tailored to their specific circumstances.

In many cities, anonymous support groups modeled after Alcoholics Anonymous, like Gamblers Anonymous (GA), play a crucial role in the recovery process. These groups offer a safe space for individuals to share their experiences and challenges without fear of judgment. The power of these gatherings lies in their communal aspect, allowing participants to draw strength from others who have walked similar paths. In the warmth of mutual understanding, many find courage they didn't know they had.

Furthermore, helplines operated by gambling addiction services provide immediate assistance, offering a vital connection to support when it's most needed. These services can be accessed anonymously and often operate 24/7, ensuring help is available whenever the urge to gamble surfaces. They serve as an entry point for further assistance, guiding individuals toward more comprehensive resources.

Besides direct intervention resources, educational workshops and seminars also form part of the broader community strategy to tackle gambling addiction. These sessions aim to increase awareness of the risks associated with gambling and the signs of addiction, both for individuals who gamble and those around them. Awareness is a preventive tool, empowering individuals with the knowledge to make informed choices about their gambling behavior.

The internet has also expanded access to help, with online platforms providing a wealth of resources. Online therapy and counseling services have grown in popularity, offering flexibility and anonymity to those who might feel uncomfortable seeking help in person. This digital realm provides forums and chat rooms to connect with others for emotional support and shared experiences.

Family plays a vital role in the recovery journey. Encouragement from loved ones can make a significant difference in helping individuals seek and stick with treatment programs. Family interventions can be an invaluable resource, although they should be approached with sensitivity and often under the guidance of a professional. Constructive support from family members can help rebuild relationships strained by gambling addiction and provide a network of support that bolsters the individual's commitment to recovery.

Financial counseling can also be a crucial component of community resources for helping those with gambling addiction. Many find themselves entangled in financial difficulties due to their gambling habits. Financial advisors who specialize in working with individuals facing debt from gambling can help develop a manageable plan to regain financial stability, offering practical steps out of debt and helping restore a sense of control over one's life.

Another important aspect of finding help is cultural sensitivity and inclusivity in available resources. People from different backgrounds experience gambling and addiction uniquely, shaped by cultural views and societal expectations. Thus, accessing culturally appropriate support can enhance the recovery process by addressing culturally specific triggers and barriers to seeking help. This diversity in service provision ensures that everyone, regardless of their background, can find help that aligns with their personal and cultural values.

While finding and utilizing resources is an essential step, maintaining engagement with these resources is equally important. Consistency can be a challenge, particularly during times when motivation wanes or external pressures mount. Here, the supportive community established through various groups and forums can provide encouragement and accountability, often acting as a buffer against relapse.

Finally, the involvement of policymakers and community leaders in promoting and supporting resources for gambling addiction can't be understated. Initiatives at this structural level, including funding for treatment facilities and campaigns promoting responsible gambling, contribute significantly to making help more accessible to those in need. Robust policy frameworks ensure that support systems are not just available but sustained over time, reflecting a community's commitment to help its members.

Finding help for gambling addiction involves navigating a complex array of resources and methods. It's a journey that requires courage, determination, and the support of a community committed to change. Through the combined effort of individuals, families, professional services, and community initiatives, those affected by gambling addiction can find the hope and help they need to reclaim their lives.

Building Support Networks

Understanding and battling gambling addiction requires more than just individual willpower; it necessitates a network of support that is strong yet adaptable. At the heart of successful recovery lies the intricate web of connections with family, friends, support groups, and professionals, all of whom play pivotal roles in guiding someone through their journey. Forming this network isn't merely about reaching out; it's about creating meaningful bonds that provide both emotional scaffolding and practical tools for change.

A vital aspect of building support networks is the sense of shared experience and understanding that they foster. Services that bring individuals together, whether through community groups or online forums, provide a platform for sharing stories and strategies. When people hear about others' journeys, they often find reflections of their own, which can validate their feelings and choices. This communal sharing not only reduces the isolation that often accompanies addiction but also serves as a wellspring of motivation and hope.

Family and close friends form the foundation of any support network. Their role is double-edged—providing both a safety net and sometimes an unintended source of pressure. For families, understanding the complexity of gambling addiction is crucial. They need support, too, in learning how to navigate the fine line between aiding recovery and enabling destructive behaviors. Open communication channels, where family members and loved ones can express concerns, share encouragement, and set boundaries, are essential for nurturing these pivotal relationships.

The involvement of professional guidance, such as therapists and counselors, adds another layer to the support network. These professionals bring an objective perspective, offering strategies based on research and clinical experience. Their interventions might range from cognitive behavioral techniques to stress management practices.

By integrating professional support with personal networks, people struggling with gambling addiction can have access to comprehensive care that addresses not only the addiction itself but also underlying issues like anxiety or depression that often accompany it.

Peer support groups provide a unique and indispensable resource in the fight against gambling addiction. Unlike familial or professional support, peer groups bring together individuals who have walked a similar path. Having someone who understands the highs and lows of addiction firsthand creates a powerful bond. Groups such as Gamblers Anonymous operate under the principle of shared experiences, facilitating a space where honesty is encouraged, and accountability is a mutual goal. The group dynamic can also inspire confidence, showing new members that recovery is not only possible but sustainable.

Online communities have increasingly become pivotal components of support networks. For individuals who are geographically isolated or hesitant to seek help in person, online forums and support groups offer anonymity and accessibility, enabling participation from the comfort of one's home. It's important for such platforms to be well-moderated to ensure a positive and constructive environment, as online interactions come with their own set of challenges and advantages.

In creating a support network, accessibility and diversity of resources are crucial. It's not simply about accumulating contacts but about ensuring these connections are appropriate and responsive to an individual's evolving needs. What works during the early stages of recovery might need adjustment as the person progresses. Therefore, networks should be fluid, ready to accommodate changes and integrate new resources as necessary.

Community organizations also play a fundamental role in building support networks. By offering educational workshops and free resources, they help reduce the stigma associated with gambling addiction and spread awareness about available help. Their resources can range from informational pamphlets to opportunities for volunteering; these avenues not only educate but also empower individuals, fostering a sense of agency and self-efficacy.

Moreover, cultural sensitivity within support networks can't be overstated. Since gambling behavior can be influenced by cultural norms and societal expectations, it's essential that support networks respect and integrate these nuances. This might involve connecting individuals with community leaders or practitioners who understand these cultural dynamics, ensuring that the support offered is truly relevant and empathetic.

Support networks should also encourage physical activities and hobbies as part of their approach. Engaging in new activities can help redirect focus and build a healthier routine, reducing the time and mental energy spent on gambling. Group activities, whether rooted in fitness, the arts, or education, can also serve as bonding experiences, reinforcing the individual's commitment to positive change while cultivating new friendships.

Ultimately, the success of a support network hinges on the strength and sincerity of its connections. It's about the quality of support just as much as the quantity. Those in recovery need a network that encourages them to be honest about their struggles, celebrates their victories, and is steadfast during setbacks. A healthy support network transforms the daunting path of recovery into one that is navigable and hopeful, recursively building on the very principles it seeks to instill.

In summary, building robust support networks is a fundamental strategy in combating gambling addiction. It requires a harmonious blend of personal, professional, communal, and cultural resources, all intertwined to provide guidance and strength. As these networks evolve, they don't just support recovery—they enrich lives and inspire change, becoming a testament to the power of community and connection.

Chapter 25:
Final Thoughts on Change

Change is both inevitable and transformative, offering a beacon of hope for individuals grappling with gambling addiction. As we stand at the crossroads of understanding and action, embracing new beginnings becomes not merely an option but a necessity. This journey towards recovery is often tumultuous, marked by moments of triumph interwoven with setbacks. However, it's important to recognize that each step forward, however small, contributes to a larger tapestry of healing and growth. The road to change demands resilience, yet it is illuminated by the prospect of a future unburdened by the shackles of addiction. By fostering an environment where acceptance of change is encouraged and embraced, society can open the door to profound transformation. The psychology of gambling addiction reveals not only the complexities of human behavior but also the boundless potential for change inherent within us all, serving as a testament to the enduring human spirit. In moving forward, there's a need for collective commitment—professionals, communities, and individuals alike—to continue exploring innovative approaches in support of sustainable change, allowing hope to flourish and guide each person towards a healthier, more fulfilling life.

Embracing New Beginnings

In the journey of understanding and overcoming gambling addiction, "Embracing New Beginnings" serves as a pivotal point. The notion of new beginnings often evokes a sense of hope and optimism. It speaks volumes about human resilience and the capacity to change, even when the shadows of addiction have loomed large for so long. This section aims to explore how individuals bravely take steps toward transformation, redefining their identities and rebuilding their lives from the ground up.

For many, the hardest part of battling gambling addiction is making the first move towards recovery. That initial step is fraught with fear and uncertainty, often laden with self-doubt. It's a leap into the unknown, where the familiarity of destructive patterns feels deceptively comforting. This process requires a shift in mindset, a deep internal commitment to oneself, and a desire to envision a future free from the shackles of gambling. It involves recognizing one's vulnerabilities not as weaknesses but as opportunities for growth.

Psychologically, embracing new beginnings can unleash a whirlwind of emotions. Feelings of relief and liberation might intermingle with sadness for loved ones' betrayals, guilt for past mistakes, or even mourning for the time lost to addiction. Acknowledging these emotions, rather than suppressing them, is crucial for healing. Emotional honesty opens the door to authentic recovery, laying a foundation for a healthier psyche and, subsequently, a healthier life.

Moreover, new beginnings often involve rewriting one's narrative. This is about changing the storyline from one of pain and loss to one of hope and courage. In this process, individuals may find themselves redefining their sense of self, exploring interests outside the realm of gambling, and discovering a newfound appreciation for life's subtleties that were previously overshadowed by addiction. This is not about erasing the past but integrating it, learning from it, and using those lessons as stepping stones toward positive change.

The support of a compassionate community plays an instrumental role in assisting individuals to embrace these new beginnings. Evidence suggests that connection is a powerful linchpin in recovery. Engaging with those who empathize and lend understanding—whether through therapy, support groups, or family ties—creates a safety net that catches individuals when they falter and lifts them when they're ready to fly again. Humans are inherently social beings, and creating robust, supportive networks can significantly impact the recovery journey.

Additionally, embarking on a new beginning often necessitates the exploration of new coping mechanisms and routines. For those who have used gambling as an emotional escape or a way to fill an emotional void, finding alternative outlets becomes essential. Engaging in physical activities, developing mindfulness practices, or nurturing creative pursuits can provide healthy escapism and emotional expression, which previously manifested through gambling. Equipping oneself with these tools not only reinforces personal resilience but also fortifies one's ability to handle the stresses and challenges that life will invariably present.

At the core of embracing a new beginning is the element of hope. It functions as a beacon, guiding individuals through the toughest times and reminding them of the potential that awaits beyond the horizon. Hope ignites the possibility of change; it nurtures ambition for a better life. It's about seeing oneself not as a 'gambler,' but as a person capable of meaningful change.

In a broader context, the narrative of new beginnings isn't limited to individuals alone. It extends to communities and society as a whole. As awareness around gambling addiction grows, so too does the collective effort to create environments that reduce harm and limit exposure to gambling's temptations. Communities can become catalysts for change, advocating for policies that support recovery and prevent addiction, thereby fostering places where new beginnings can flourish for everyone involved.

In conclusion, embracing new beginnings in the context of gambling addiction is not merely about halting destructive behaviors; it's a comprehensive realignment of mind, body, and soul. It's a courageous journey of self-discovery and empowerment. This section underscores the importance of individual and communal transformation, reinforcing the belief that while the path to recovery is arduous, it is also immensely rewarding. With every new beginning comes the promise of untapped potential, the unyielding power of hope, and the infinite possibility of a renewed future.

Hope for the Future

Change is often daunting, particularly when it involves breaking free from the grip of gambling addiction. Yet, within the heart of change lies opportunity, a chance to redefine identity and goals. The road to recovery is laden with challenges, but it's also a path of profound transformation. This journey isn't just about leaving something behind but also about moving towards something promising and new—hope for the future.

One of the most compelling aspects of hope lies in its ability to inspire action, even when the odds seem stacked against us. Science has shown that hope is not just an abstract concept but a significant predictor of positive outcomes in treatment. It inspires motivation and persistence, essential ingredients for overcoming the hurdles that arise throughout the recovery process. When individuals suffering from gambling addiction harbor hope, they begin to envisage possibilities beyond their current circumstances, envisioning a healthier and more fulfilling future.

Hope acts as a catalyst for mental shifts, altering perceptions and guiding behaviors away from destructive habits and towards constructive ones. It encourages openness to new experiences, whether it's trying new therapies, engaging with support groups, or exploring alternative outlets for enjoyment. There's an undeniable power in sharing stories of recovery, where hope plays a pivotal role. These narratives not only motivate the storyteller to continue their journey but also offer a beacon of light to others who feel entrapped by addiction.

Community and connection significantly contribute to hope's growth. Isolation often accompanies addiction, drawing a veil over possibilities for change. However, bringing addiction to light through communities of support alters that narrative. Finding a network of understanding, compassionate individuals fosters hope. This communal strength can amplify one's resolve to seek improvement and renew focus on long-term recovery goals.

Education and awareness are equally instrumental in fortifying hope for those grappling with gambling addiction. Knowledge empowers individuals with the tools they need to fight against dependency. Understanding the psychological and physiological mechanisms of addiction provides clarity and direction, transforming perceived weaknesses into areas of strength and development. As individuals learn to navigate their triggers and responses, they derive hope from the fact that they possess the ability to change their trajectory.

Moreover, society plays a crucial role in instilling hope by dismantling the stigma surrounding gambling addiction. Acceptance frees individuals to acknowledge their struggles without judgment, thereby creating a more honest dialogue about seeking help and support. When society views addiction through a lens of compassion and understanding, it encourages both individuals and their families to confront the issue head-on, promoting healing and long-lasting change.

Advancements in technology and research offer additional hope for the future. Innovative treatment methods and predictive tools are being developed, providing tailored interventions and early detection of potential problems. These advances make recovery more accessible and effective, offering renewed optimism for prevention and relapse prevention strategies. As technology becomes an ally in battling addiction, it signals a promising shift towards more personalized and successful recovery journeys.

Multifaceted commitment from policymakers, healthcare providers, and communities promises a more supportive environment for recovery. Changes in legislation and regulation focused on ethical gambling practices ensure that people are protected from exploitation and harm. This commitment underscores the importance of a collective effort in sustaining hope and funneling it towards meaningful societal change.

The path of recovery is uniquely challenging, tangled with personal demons and societal pressures. However, what makes the journey rewarding is the emergence of new perspectives, goals, and well-being. Embracing change does more than conquer addiction; it leads to discoveries about oneself and the world, painting a picture of a life where the present is not dictated by past dependencies.

Hope for the future gives individuals the courage to rebuild relationships, pursue neglected dreams, and foster new passions. It encourages them to envision a life punctuated not by the chase of fleeting thrills but by meaningful and sustained fulfillment. It offers reassurance that, though the path to recovery might be fraught with setbacks, each step forward is a step towards a brighter future.

As the grip of addiction loosens and hope takes root, individuals can appreciate life beyond the constraints of gambling, where emotions are genuine, relationships are restored, and achievements resonate with personal significance. Invariably, it's this hope that spurs enduring change, redefining one's place in the world and opening the door to endless possibilities. While the struggle may continue, it's the hope for the future that provides the power to persist through adversity, transforming lives and societies alike.

Conclusion

In reflecting upon the complex tapestry of gambling addiction, it's evident that the journey toward understanding and mitigating this condition is as intricate as the forces that pull individuals into its grasp. Throughout this book, we've explored the psychological, social, and physiological elements that contribute to the allure of gambling, a phenomenon that goes beyond mere games of chance. The interplay of these factors creates a compelling narrative about human behavior, resilience, and the continual search for meaning in the face of uncertainty.

At its core, gambling addiction serves as a lens through which we can examine broader societal issues. Fundamentally, the thrill of risk and reward taps into our most basic psychological impulses, deeply embedded within the brain's reward system. This system, while designed to enhance survival through well-regulated pleasure, can malfunction when faced with the distortions of chance that gambling presents. The dopamine pathways that reward our pursuits become maladaptive, driving behaviors that resemble drug addiction. Yet, this doesn't fully encapsulate the individual stories and struggles that accompany these biological mechanisms. Each person's experience with gambling is as unique as the myriad elements that contribute to their addiction.

The various chapters of this book have touched upon cultural, technological, and emotional aspects that add crucial depth to our understanding. Culture dictates not only how gambling is viewed but also how it's practiced and perceived across different societies. The digital age has made gambling more accessible, raising the stakes with the advent of online platforms that can amplify both the risk and reach of gambling behaviors. Emotional voids left unaddressed can make individuals more susceptible to seeking solace in gambling, highlighting the importance of awareness of these triggers for prevention and recovery.

Individual agency, the capacity to make choices and exert power over one's lifestyle decisions, plays a pivotal role in recovery. The stages of change detailed in this book remind us that recovery is a journey, one that requires perseverance, support, and sometimes the reinvention of self. Relapse isn't a sign of failure but a potential learning point on the path to a sustainable lifestyle change. Efforts in therapy and support groups offer frameworks for combining this personal agency with proven strategies for change. It's a testament to resilience and the capacity for growth that defines the human spirit.

Family and society are powerful forces that can significantly influence recovery and resistance to gambling's pull. As chapters have shown, when families unite and provide unyielding support, they become pillars of strength in the fight against addiction. The role of education, prevention, and policy in addressing gambling addiction cannot be overstated. These elements work in concert to create awareness and provide resources, aiming to curtail the burgeoning tide of gambling addiction. Effective legislation and responsible gambling practices are necessary tools to safeguard communities and ensure accountability.

In contemplating future directions, the potential of technological advances in predictive tools and personalized recovery plans offers promise. These innovations could spearhead a new wave of preventive measures, encouraging timely interventions before gambling behaviors escalate to harmful levels. Research also holds the key to unraveling more nuances in gambling addiction, providing insights that could fuel new treatment methodologies and deepen our comprehension of this multifaceted issue.

Stories of recovery, peppered throughout, remind us of the human capacity to overcome adversity. They are not just narratives of personal triumph but are illuminating testimonies that offer hope to others. Gambling addiction, like many compulsions, isn't isolated to individuals; it weaves through family units, communities, and ultimately society itself. In sharing these stories, a collective strength can emerge, reinforcing the notion that recovery is possible and support networks are vital.

At the heart of preventing and overcoming gambling addiction is a call for ethical consideration and industry responsibility. As we look forward, these elements become crucial in shaping a more conscious and caring society. Addressing moral dilemmas and holding industry to standards that prioritize wellbeing over profit are steps toward lasting change. The balance between freedom of choice and protective oversight often presents a challenging ethical landscape that demands ongoing dialogue and reflection.

In conclusion, the fight against gambling addiction is perennial and multidimensional. But as complex as these challenges are, so too is the resilience of those who rise above them. The insights gleaned throughout this exploration are not just a culmination but a springboard for action. It's a call to embrace change, foster resilience, and cultivate hope for the future. As we move forward, we are reminded that each step toward understanding and recovery brings us closer to a society where everyone has the opportunity to thrive, unburdened by the chains of gambling addiction.

Appendix A:
Appendix

As we wrap up our exploration of the multifaceted world of gambling addiction, this appendix serves as a guiding beacon, offering readers additional resources and avenues for further enrichment. Diving into the depths of gambling psychology, it paves pathways to understand the underlying complexities and offers material for those eager to delve deeper into the nuances beyond the pages of this book. The curated selection of further reading, support networks, and resourceful tools provides both a bridge to informed curiosity and a roadmap to fostering resilience against the allure of gambling. Herein lies a collection designed to empower, educate, and encourage proactive steps toward embracing knowledge and healing, for both those affected by gambling addiction and the professionals dedicated to helping them. As knowledge expands the horizon of understanding, it also opens the door to recovery and prevention, ensuring that the journey leads not just to insight but also to meaningful change.

Additional Resources

In the journey to understanding and addressing gambling addiction, accessing a well-rounded set of resources can be a game-changer. These resources offer further insights, practical tools, and community support, vital for those struggling with addiction and those looking to lend a hand. While this book sheds light on various psychological and emotional aspects of gambling, the following resources provide additional support and information to deepen understanding and facilitate recovery.

For those who find themselves in the trenches of gambling addiction, support groups such as *Gamblers Anonymous* have proven invaluable. Modeled after the successful framework of Alcoholics Anonymous, Gamblers Anonymous provides a fellowship for individuals to share their experiences and support one another in a non-judgmental environment. This program emphasizes personal responsibility and the power of communal support, aiming to help individuals regain control of their lives.

There are also numerous online platforms and forums dedicated to those affected by gambling addiction. Websites such as *Gambling Therapy* and *BeGambleAware* offer confidential support, live discussions, and comprehensive resources tailored to help individuals understand and navigate their addiction. These platforms often have a global reach, widening their accessibility and impact.

For professionals seeking to expand their knowledge on the topic, several research outlets and online databases provide in-depth articles and studies. Journals like the *Journal of Gambling Issues* and the *International Gambling Studies* offer peer-reviewed research, keeping readers informed of the latest developments and insights in the field of gambling studies. These sources are indispensable for psychologists, counselors, and other professionals striving to stay current with treatment methodologies and theoretical advancements.

In addition to academic sources, books penned by experts can offer a robust understanding of gambling addiction from various perspectives. Authors like Natasha Dow Schüll, who wrote *"Addiction by Design: Machine Gambling in Las Vegas"*, delve into the systemic issues surrounding gambling, enriching readers' perspectives with in-depth analysis and personal anecdotes. Such works often provide a more nuanced understanding of the intricate web of motivations and consequences entwined in gambling behaviors.

Educational courses and workshops, available both online and in person, are also valuable resources. Institutions such as the *National Council on Problem Gambling* offer programs that educate individuals on the risks associated with gambling, teaching preventative strategies and coping mechanisms. These courses target both individuals susceptible to addiction and professionals endeavoring to offer interventions.

In recent years, technological advancements have presented new tools and applications to aid in the fight against gambling addiction. Mobile apps like *Bettor Time* are designed to monitor gambling habits and provide users with real-time data on their activities, including time spent and money wagered. Such tools serve as a constant reminder and deterrent, encouraging responsible behavior through transparency.

Community-based initiatives play a significant role, too. Many communities have developed local support groups and peer-led initiatives, offering face-to-face support for those grappling with gambling addiction. These community resources foster an environment of accountability and encouragement, ensuring that those in recovery are never isolated in their efforts.

For those interested in policy and advocacy, organizations such as *Stop Predatory Gambling* work towards changing societal attitudes and governments' roles in enabling gambling addiction. By focusing on legislative change and public awareness, such organizations strive to create a long-lasting preventative impact on communities worldwide.

Internet resources have also expanded to provide family and friends of gamblers with tools and information necessary to support their loved ones. Resources like the *Family Toolkit* from GamCare provide guidance on approaching conversations about gambling, recognizing signs of addiction, and accessing professional advice. Support for family members is crucial, as their roles can significantly influence the recovery journey.

Lastly, podcasts and webinars offer an accessible and often engaging way to learn about gambling addiction. Series such as *"All In: The Addicted Gambler's Podcast"* offer listener-friendly content with expert interviews, sharing stories of struggle and triumph. These platforms have the power to reach new audiences by discussing the complexities of addiction in relatable and inspiring ways.

Each of these resources provides a unique contribution to understanding and combating gambling addiction, offering hope, guidance, and knowledge. By leveraging these tools, individuals and professionals alike can foster a deeper connection to the issue, creating pathways for recovery and effective intervention strategies. The fight against gambling addiction is multifaceted, and these resources ensure that support is diverse and widely accessible, shaping a future where more individuals achieve freedom from the grips of addiction.

Further Reading

As you deepen your understanding of the complexities surrounding gambling addiction, it becomes increasingly valuable to explore a wide array of scholarly works and resources. This further reading section acts as a compass, guiding you toward enriching texts that will enhance the knowledge you've already gleaned from this book.

One indispensable starting point is to delve into the psychological intricacies that drive gambling behavior. Books such as "Addiction by Design" by Natasha Dow Schüll explore the intersection between human psychology and machine design. Schüll's research provides a compelling look into how the architecture of slot machines can exploit the human brain's reward system, making it difficult for individuals to disengage.

To gain a comprehensive grasp of the neurological foundations of gambling addiction, consider perusing Mark D. Griffiths's various works on the psychological elements of gambling. Griffiths' extensive research into the psychobiology of gambling offers insight into how gambling can hijack the brain's reward mechanisms, providing a bridge between psychological theories and real-world applications. His studies are pivotal for anyone interested in the cognitive processes that make gambling so compelling.

Diving into the realm of recovery, Howard J. Shaffer's research presents valuable insights into therapeutic approaches that have shown promise in treating gambling addiction. His work often highlights the importance of cognitive-behavioral strategies and provides evidence-based guidance for clinicians. Coupled with motivational interviews and group counseling techniques, Shaffer's contributions can aid those looking to understand or facilitate the recovery journey.

Additionally, for a broad overview of the sociocultural factors influencing gambling behavior, you might turn to collective works on cross-cultural gambling implications. Authors and researchers in this field often examine historical and cultural contexts, offering a lens through which we can understand why gambling takes different forms across societies. Such analyses are critical for grasping the nuanced ways in which cultural identity influences gambling tendencies.

Peer-reviewed journals are another pivotal resource for those seeking cutting-edge research. Publications like the "Journal of Gambling Studies" and "International Gambling Studies" regularly feature the latest scientific studies, offering a wealth of data and theoretical advances that are significant for both academics and practitioners in behavioral sciences.

If you're more interested in the ethical aspects and policy implications of gambling, examining works that focus on regulation and industry practices can be enlightening. Some authors provide critical assessments of current legislation and propose frameworks for ethical gambling, tackling issues like advertising restrictions and the responsibilities of the gambling industry.

The digital realm, too, is bursting with resources. E-books, articles, and online courses hosted by prominent universities often cover the numerous dimensions of gambling and its societal impact. Websites dedicated to addiction studies frequently offer free resources, including toolkits and webinars from experts in the field.

It's also essential to acknowledge the voices of those who've been directly affected by gambling addiction. Personal accounts and autobiographies serve as poignant reminders of the human cost of addiction. These narratives can be profoundly moving and sometimes offer unique insights that complement academic studies, reminding us of the real, lived experiences behind statistics and theories.

Considering prevention and policy, documents and reports from organizations such as the National Council on Problem Gambling and other internationally recognized bodies provide crucial data and policy recommendations. Their publications often analyze trends, highlight gaps in current methodologies, and propose innovative strategies for the future.

Lastly, whether you're a professional in the field or a concerned individual seeking personal understanding, staying informed about the latest research and methodologies is paramount. Continuous learning through targeted reading ensures that your knowledge remains both current and comprehensive, ultimately leading to a better understanding of gambling addiction and its far-reaching consequences.